Kakatkar

Advanced Applications of Network Analysis in Marketing Science

AF189216

ecm

Series: Electronic Commerce & Digital Markets
Volume: 7
Editor: Prof. Dr. Martin Spann
ISSN: 2199-7608

Ludwig-Maximilians-Universität München
Munich School of Management
Institute of Electronic Commerce and Digital Markets
Geschwister-Scholl-Platz 1
80539 Munich
Germany
www.ecm.bwl.lmu.de

Chinmay Kakatkar

Advanced Applications of
Network Analysis in Marketing Science

Foreword by Martin Spann

BoD – Books on Demand Verlag

Imprint

Bibliographic information is published by Deutsche Nationalbibliothek.
The Deutsche Nationalbibliothek lists this publication in the Deutsche Nationalbibliografie; detailed bibliographic data are available on the internet at http://dnb.d-nb.de.

Author:
Dr. oec. publ. Chinmay Kakatkar
E-Mail: chinmay.kakatkar@gmail.com

Production and Publishing:
BoD – Books on Demand, Norderstedt
In de Tarpen 42
22848 Norderstedt
Germany
E-Mail: info@bod.de
Internet: www.bod.de

Dissertation 2018
LMU Munich/Ludwig-Maximilians-Universität München
Reference Number/Kennziffer: D 19
Foreword by Prof. Dr. Martin Spann

1ˢᵗ Edition 2018

Cover design & layout: Dr. Chinmay Kakatkar
Cover image: © Dr. Chinmay Kakatkar

ISSN 2199-7608
ISBN 9-783746-068114

Foreword

The digitization of consumer and business interactions has provided a vast amount of digital network data. Marketing managers and researchers have benefited from this novel data source by utilizing social network analysis to exploit information about interpersonal consumer relations, e.g., to explain new product diffusion or identify seeding points for marketing campaigns.

However, the technique of network analysis has more to offer beyond analyzing consumers' social networks. First examples have been analyses of networks of joint product purchases in shopping baskets for the purpose of deriving product recommendations. Given this potential, business research needs to explore novel applications of network analysis in marketing and test their performance compared to traditional methods.

Chinmay Kakatkar's dissertation pursues this aim of analyzing methods of network analysis – in combination with complementary quantitative methods – to solve marketing science problems in product development, pricing and distribution management.

In four different studies, he shows that network analysis can help marketing managers in solving product assortment problems, identifying attributes of successful new products, predicting the success of new pricing strategies as well as analyzing consumer behavior in offline retailing.

Chinmay Kakatkar's dissertation is an important contribution to the methodological toolbox and practice of marketing science. He successfully combines techniques from computer science and marketing to real world datasets and thus demonstrates the high managerial relevance of his research. I wish that marketing science research and practice will benefit from the insights of this dissertation.

Munich, February 2018   Martin Spann

Preface and Acknowledgements

In the summer of 2015, I joined the Institute of Electronic Commerce and Digital Markets (ECM) at the Ludwig-Maximilian University of Munich as a doctoral researcher. The ECM encourages interdisciplinary research at the intersection of marketing science and technology, with a focus on topics relevant to e-commerce. Led by Prof. Dr. Martin Spann, an internationally acclaimed and well-published marketing scholar, the ECM enjoys strong connections to external partners from academia and industry. From the outset, I benefited greatly from this excellent research environment, and quickly became immersed in a number of exciting research projects that ultimately led to my doctoral dissertation.

My research at the ECM has primarily focused on advanced applications of network analysis to answer interesting questions in marketing science. At its most basic, a network is formed by a collection of entities that are connected to each other in some way. While past research in marketing has looked extensively at networks of people and large aggregate entities such as firms, my focus has been on networks at a more granular level. For example, one can construct a network of products, and even of their product features, to derive new insights about the products and their consumers. As our world becomes increasingly connected, and the notion of the Internet of Things moves from hype to reality, taking a network perspective on consumer behavior will arguably continue to gain in relevance for academics and practitioners alike. I am therefore delighted to have had the opportunity to work in this exciting domain and contribute to the research community.

Throughout my time at the ECM, I had the pleasure of working with a number of exceptional people who have guided and encouraged my research pursuit. First and foremost, I would like to thank my doctoral supervisor, Prof. Dr. Martin Spann, for his strong support and mentorship throughout. His vast theoretical and empirical knowledge of the subject matter and steadfast encouragement to carry out cutting-edge research greatly influenced the quality of my work, and deepened my appreciation of the scientific process. I would also like to thank Prof. Dr. Thomas Hess, the second referee for my dissertation, for his time and insightful feedback. I am also grateful to my colleagues at the ECM (in alphabetical order) – Camila Back, Waltraud Broch, Gabor Darvasi, Andrea Dechant, Andreas Heusler, Lena Hoeck, Katharina Massner, Philipp Nägelein, David Prakash, Emanuel Schuster, Dr. Lucas Stich, and Kamilla Zab – for making the Institute a close-knit and productive research environment.

Moreover, I had the chance to work with Prof. Dr. Johann Füller (University of Innsbruck) and Prof. Dr. Julia De Groote (University of Bern) on a research project, and wish to thank them for making our collaboration a highly enriching experience. I am also grateful to Prof. Dr. Dominik Molitor, Prof. Dr. Marc Fischer and Prof. Dr. Olivier Toubia for their helpful comments on various research projects. I also wish to thank Sven Haiges and Lars Gregori of SAP Hybris Labs, and Michael Hagemann and his team at Uni Merch GmbH, for their excellent support in the setup of a field experiment as part of an early research project.

I am indebted to my family for their continued love and support, encouraging my passion for research, and providing the moral support necessary for seeing my doctoral endeavor through to its conclusion. I am also grateful to my friends and various other amazing people from academia and industry that I have gotten to know over the years, for their insightful advice and fresh perspectives. Having spent the last few years deeply immersed in the network perspective, I would like to conclude by saying that I hope it is indeed a small world, and I look forward to working again with the fantastic people I have met so far at some point in the future.

Munich, February 2018   Chinmay Kakatkar

ADVANCED APPLICATIONS OF
NETWORK ANALYSIS IN MARKETING SCIENCE

Inaugural-Dissertation
zur Erlangung des Grades Doctor oeconomiae publicae (Dr. oec. publ.)
an der Ludwig-Maximilians-Universität München

vorgelegt von

Chinmay Ravindra Kakatkar

Jahr: 2017

Referent:	Prof. Dr. Martin Spann
Korreferent:	Prof. Dr. Thomas Hess
Promotionsabschlussberatung:	31.01.2018

Contents

11

Dissertation Overview

1. Relevance and Aim of Dissertation

The world today is becoming a highly connected place. Firms, consumers and the devices they use are increasingly part of a complex, global network of connected entities. By recent estimates, about 4 billion people now use the Internet, roughly 3 billion users (including company accounts and individual users) are active on social media platforms, and much of the growth in web traffic is driven by mobile devices (Kemp, 2017). Facebook alone has about 1 billion daily active users, and the average Facebook user has several hundred "friends" on the platform (Smith, 2016). These networks represent a gold mine for marketing scholars that may be interested in developing a better understanding of consumer behavior, and for practitioners who are keen to discover new ways of gaining and retaining customers.

The concept of a network is formally rooted in the mathematical domain of graph theory (Newman, 2010). A network is essentially a graph consisting of nodes connected by edges. Armed with these basic building blocks of nodes and edges, we can represent a vast array of relational properties observable in the real world. Historically, the study of networks in the social sciences has typically focused on the analysis of ties between individual people, and between larger collectives such as firms (Borgatti, Mehra, Brass, & Labianca, 2009). Nodes in social networks can be linked by an edge if they have some social property in common. For instance, two people may be linked because they are friends, live in the same location, or share the same opinion on a given subject. Some people may be especially well-connected within a sub-community of the network, while other people may form bridges between different sub-communities (Granovetter, 1973).

While social networks continue to hold much importance in marketing science, scholars have increasingly begun to expand the scope of network analysis to other types of nodes and edges that may represent fruitful areas of research. For example, recent studies suggest that retailers can gain useful insights into the purchase-related behavior of customers by considering a network representation of the product assortment (Raeder & Chawla, 2009; Videla-Cavieres & Rios, 2014). Similar products may share a tie in a product network, and the information about a product's position and connectedness in the network can feed into the retailer's product recommendation algorithm (Xiao & Benbasat, 2007). A network also allows the representation of "path data" in marketing, such as that generated by the movement of shoppers within and between stores (Hui, Fader, & Bradlow, 2009).

Recognizing the value of the information stored in today's data-rich environments, scholars have become more vocal in their calls for further research that extends our knowledge of methods for analyzing new forms of data (Bradlow, Gangwar, Kopalle, & Voleti, 2017; Wedel & Kannan, 2016). In this spirit, the following cumulative dissertation focuses on the use of network analysis to generate and analyze novel data in marketing. The work moves beyond the scope of traditional social network analysis to consider networks composed of different types of nodes at varying levels of granularity. The key aim of expanding the scope of analysis in this manner is to demonstrate that network analysis can be used to investigate novel explanatory and outcome variables that hold contextual meaning and can deepen our understanding of the research question at hand. The essays in this dissertation showcase a selection of advanced applications of network analysis in marketing science that are arguably of value to scholars and practitioners alike.

2. Structure of Cumulative Dissertation

The dissertation consists of four essays. Table 1 provides an overview of each essay in terms of the research question, methodology and data used. While the specific research question and data sources vary across the essays, the common thread throughout the cumulative dissertation is the advanced use of network analysis – in combination with other techniques from domains such as econometrics and machine learning – to extend our understanding of consumer behavior in marketing science.

Essay 1 starts with the observation that retail customers are known to sometimes engage in complex "customer projects" that are reflected by a series of purchases that span several shopping trips and store locations over a period of time. The fragmented nature of these purchases makes it particularly difficult to identify customer projects accurately. A predictive methodology is developed based on product networks to tackle this problem. Essays 2 and 3 are broadly concerned with marketing questions surrounding the development and launch of new products. By recasting product ideas as networks of their constituent features, these essays ask whether there is something about the idea itself that might correlate with outcome variables of interest. Finally, Essay 4 is motivated by the recognition that event data (especially data collected by physical sensors) that does not track individuals exactly is still relatively under-researched in marketing science, but gaining in practical importance with the advent of the Internet of Things. A network-based method is developed to address key challenges in the analysis of such event data, including the inability to always identify individual consumers precisely and the difficulty of deriving contextually meaningful predictor and outcome variables to assess the performance of marketing strategies.

Essays	Research Questions	Methodology and Data
1. A Network Perspective on Identifying Customer Projects C. Kakatkar (single-author essay)	How effective are relational measures derived from product networks in identifying customer projects?	Formalized the problem of identifying customer projects; Carried out network analysis at the level of products to derive network-based methods of predicting project membership; Used best-seller lists and collaborative filtering as benchmark methods; Combined network-based and benchmark methods to analyze complementarity between them. Used data on customer purchase histories from a retailer in the UK (N = 538,993 transactions) and in Taiwan (N = 817,741 transactions) to test predictive algorithms.
2. The DNA of Winning Ideas - A Network Perspective of Success in New Product Development C. Kakatkar, J. de Groote, J. Füller and M. Spann	To what extent can the ingredients of a new product idea – and the measures derived from the related ingredient network – accurately predict the idea's success?	Represented ideas for new products as a shared network of contextually meaningful idea features, based on a theoretically founded configurational view of the idea itself; Derived idea-level network measures of feature centrality and community structure; Used machine learning to build a network-based algorithm to predict idea success; Conducted further exploratory analyses and estimated additional Probit models to check robustness of findings. Used idea-level data from an online idea competition in the consumer goods sector (N = 468 ideas) to validate the network-based predictors of idea success, where success is measured by the expert jury rating available in the dataset.
3. Dynamic Pricing of New Products - The Effects of Strategic Momentum and Feature Composition C. Kakatkar and M. Spann	What is the link between the dynamic pricing strategy of a new product, the product's feature network, and the pricing strategy of the product's predecessor?	Derived a network of product features from a given specification of a product's feature composition; Derived a fuzzy mapping between products and their immediate predecessors in the product series; Specified Probit models with the dynamic pricing strategy of a product as the outcome variable, and two sets of correlates, namely the pricing strategy of the predecessor, and measures of feature core-ness and breadth derived from the feature network. Used a dataset of new product launches in the market for cameras in a large European country (N = 663 products launched) to test the Probit models.
4. Analyzing Consumer Behavior with Non-Tracking Event Data C. Kakatkar and M. Spann	To what extent can a network perspective help us analyze consumer behavior in online and offline retail settings using event data that does not track individual consumers precisely?	Developed a three-step method to analyze non-tracking event data: (1) Approximate the identification of individuals from event streams using a temporal, spatial or other/ combined slicing heuristic based on a guided or unguided approach, (2) Derive contextually meaningful outcome variables (by constructing composite conditional probabilities of event transitions) and predictor variables (especially based on a network representation of artifacts in the retail setting), (3) Build classification and regression models linking the outcome and predictor variables. Used event data from a randomized field experiment that generated customer-product interaction events (N = 3,106 events), which were captured by deploying sensor-enabled shelves in a merchandising store of a large European university.

Table 1: Overview of Dissertation Essays

3. Implications for Marketing Science and Practice

The essays that form this dissertation lead to some key implications for marketing scholars. First and foremost, the essays highlight the versatility of the network perspective in marketing science beyond the social dimension (Wasserman & Faust, 1994). Each essay shows how the basic building blocks of a network – namely its nodes and edges – can be derived and used in a variety of ways. For instance, while the network in Essay 1 is constructed at the level of whole products, Essays 2 and 3 go deeper by building networks of product features.

Secondly, building on the concepts of the preceding essays, Essay 4 underscores the value of combining networks composed of different entity types (events and environmental artifacts, in our case) into a single, cohesive model of consumer behavior. Essay 4 shows that recasting event streams that appear to have limited raw informational value into networks can yield fruitful variables to represent interesting outcomes and predictors. The implication of jointly considering multi-type nodes thus complements extant literature that models different types of ties in a single network (Ansari, Koenigsberg, & Stahl, 2011).

Thirdly, the essays point to the novel research opportunities created by shifting the focus away from individuals – as is common in marketing science – to the relationships between individual entities and the structure of the network that they form (Borgatti et al., 2009). Crucially, the networks constructed in each essay are really several different networks superimposed onto a single network of common nodes and ties. For example, whereas each customer project in Essay 1 is approximated by only some of the products co-occurring in the purchase histories of individual customers, the full network used for identifying customer projects superimposes all of these project-level networks into a single product network. Similarly, Essays 2 and 3 merge several idea- or product-based networks of features into a single feature network, and Essay 4 superimposes smaller networks defined by the heuristic for slicing event streams into larger networks of events and artifacts. The superimposition of networks in all of these cases implies an overarching, shared "DNA" that describes commonalities and differences across entities such as projects, products and event streams in a given context.

The essays also yield some important implications for practitioners of marketing and innovation. The much-hyped "fourth industrial revolution" of automation, hyper-connection and artificial intelligence is fast becoming a reality (Schwab, 2017). Data is constantly being generated and firms increasingly have the technological means to store, analyze and transform the wealth of data to derive commercially relevant insights (Bradlow et al., 2017). Firms are consequently beginning to prepare for the impending disruption of the status quo by building capabilities and resources that support advanced analytics. As our essays indicate, firms can benefit from considering network-based methods alongside other methods that derive from econometrics and various strands of machine learning (Varian, 2014). However, discussions with practitioners during the course of this doctoral research suggest that there is currently limited understanding of the untapped value of network analysis among decision-makers within firms. Harnessing the power of networks can thus become a significant competitive advantage for firms that are willing to make the necessary investments in talent and technology.

More generally, the versatility of network analysis means that it is useful to marketing practitioners across industries and subject domains. A consumer's decisions can be analyzed using representations of mental associative networks, for example, while the search and selection of products can be viewed through the kinds of networks that are showcased in this dissertation (Dhar, Geva, Oestreicher-Singer, & Sundararajan, 2014; Schwab, 2017). Networks are thus ideally suited to capture and derive commercial value from the different aspects of consumer behavior in the modern world.

References

Ansari, A., Koenigsberg, O., & Stahl, F. (2011). Modeling multiple relationships in social networks. *Journal of Marketing Research, 48*(4), 713–728.

Borgatti, S. P., Mehra, A., Brass, D. J., & Labianca, G. (2009). Network analysis in the social sciences. *Science, 323*(5916), 892–895.

Bradlow, E. T., Gangwar, M., Kopalle, P., & Voleti, S. (2017). The role of big data and predictive analytics in retailing. *Journal of Retailing, 93*(1), 79–95.

Dhar, V., Geva, T., Oestreicher-Singer, G., & Sundararajan, A. (2014). Prediction in economic networks. *Information Systems Research, 25*(2), 264–284.

Granovetter, M. S. (1973). The strength of weak ties. *American Journal of Sociology, 78*(6), 1360–1380.

Hui, S. K., Fader, P. S., & Bradlow, E. T. (2009). Path data in marketing: An integrative framework and prospectus for model building. *Marketing Science, 28*(2), 320–335.

Kemp, S. (2017). *The global state of the internet in April 2017.* Retrieved from https://thenextweb.com/contributors/2017/04/11/current-global-state-internet/#.tnw_aNf5x7mM

Newman, M. (2010). *Networks: An introduction.* New York: Oxford University Press.

Raeder, T., & Chawla, N. V. (2009). Modeling a store's product space as a social network. In *Social Network Analysis and Mining, 2009. ASONAM'09. International Conference on Advances in* (pp. 164–169).

Schwab, K. (2017). *The Fourth Industrial Revolution.* New York: Random House Inc.

Smith, K. (2016). *Marketing: 47 Facebook Statistics for 2016.* Retrieved from https://www.brandwatch.com/blog/47-facebook-statistics-2016/

Varian, H. R. (2014). Big data: New tricks for econometrics. *The Journal of Economic Perspectives, 28*(2), 3–27.

Videla-Cavieres, I. F., & Rios, S. A. (2014). Extending market basket analysis with graph mining techniques: A real case. *Expert Systems with Applications, 41*(4), 1928–1936.

Wasserman, S., & Faust, K. (1994). *Social Network Analysis: Methods and Applications* (Vol. 8): Cambridge University Press.

Wedel, M., & Kannan, P. K. (2016). Marketing analytics for data-rich environments. *Journal of Marketing, 80*(6), 97–121.

Xiao, B., & Benbasat, I. (2007). E-commerce product recommendation agents: use characteristics and impact. *MIS Quarterly, 31*(1), 137–209.

Essay 1:

A Network Perspective on Identifying Customer Projects

Chinmay Kakatkar

Abstract

In the retail context, a "customer project" can be defined as a complex endeavor by a customer that involves purchasing a set of products to achieve a certain goal within a given timeframe (e.g., organizing a large dinner or renovating a house). Knowing whether a customer is currently engaged in a project – and if so, the nature of that project – can help inform a retailer's marketing strategy. Identifying customer projects via typically available forms of transaction data is not a straightforward task. Purchases related to a given project may span multiple shopping trips, rendering simple basket analyses insufficient. We present a methodology that applies network analysis to historical product purchase data to approximate the identification of projects across product categories and store formats. The procedure is scalable and can be integrated into existing data analytics solutions used by retailers. We empirically test the methodology with two sample datasets from the field. Our findings suggest that the network-based concepts of tie strength and community structure tend to be statistically significant and complementary predictors of project composition. We also show that such network-based methods can build on other established methods such as best-seller lists and collaborative filtering to achieve a higher combined predictive accuracy. Based on our findings, retailers can arguably enhance their ability to recommend relevant products or product bundles to customers by complementing existing customer data analytics with network analyses of project-based purchase patterns.

Keywords: Customer Projects, Network Analysis, Predictive Modeling, Retail Marketing

1. Introduction

A happily married couple, Sally and Bob, are about to move into a new residence and have started making plans for their house-warming party. The couple is planning to invite their friends and new neighbors over for dinner and show everyone around the house. As such, the dinner menu must be finalized and the required ingredients need to be purchased. The couple is also thinking of decorating the living room and the front garden for the occasion; this could involve buying not just the decorative items themselves, but also the tools and equipment needed to properly set these up (e.g., screw drivers, cutters and so on).

The fictitious scenario described above captures some instances of what we might refer to as "customer projects", i.e., fairly complex endeavors such as organizing a large event or moving into a new home. In general, completing the project may involve shopping for items based on some materials list, and this can be seen as a form of goal-oriented purchase behavior (Grewal, Roggeveen, & Nordfält, 2016). Knowing whether a customer is currently engaged in a project (and if so, the nature of that project), can enhance a retailer's ability to recommend relevant products or product bundles to that customer. Technological advancements have increasingly enabled retailers to collect vast amounts of individual-level customer data on past purchases as well as real-time transactions (Goldenberg, 2008). These disparate data streams can be aggregated, analyzed and segmented using various data mining techniques in order to deliver actionable insights (Ngai, Xiu, & Chau, 2009). Retailers can incorporate data on project-based customer behavior to plan tailored advertisement campaigns, loyalty programs, and improve existing forms of automatic recommendation systems (Bodapati, 2008).

However, identifying customer projects via typically available forms of transaction data is not a straightforward task. Purchases related to a given project may span multiple shopping trips, rendering simple basket analyses insufficient. Moreover, all items on the materials list may not necessarily be purchased at the same store location, or even the same retailer. These information gaps may potentially give the retailer an incomplete view of the customer project, which could lead to erroneous predictions about future shopping patterns. To successfully exploit the opportunities created by project-based customer behavior, we therefore need a methodology to identify – or at least approximate – the existence of projects, in order to overcome the limitations inherent to the transaction data collected by the retailer.

By considering the problem of project identification from a network perspective, this paper makes two main contributions. First, we describe a methodology that applies network analysis to historical product purchase data to approximate the identification of projects across product categories and B2B/B2C store formats. The procedure is scalable and can be integrated into existing data analytics solutions used by retailers. Second, we empirically test the methodology with two field datasets to assess the value-add of the network-based approach. Our findings suggest that the network-based concepts of tie strength and community structure tend to be significant and complementary predictors of project composition. We also show that the network-based methods can build on other established methods such as best-seller lists and collaborative filtering to achieve a higher combined predictive accuracy. Based on our findings, retailers can arguably enhance their marketing strategies regarding product recommendations and product bundling by complementing existing customer data analytics with network analyses of project-based purchase patterns.

2. Related Literature

2.1 Conceptualizing Customer Projects

The notion of a customer project can be derived from the stream of literature based on Bagozzi and Dholakia (1999), which argues that consumer behavior may be guided by goals. Goals can be hierarchical, so that several sub-goals may build up to the fulfillment of the overall goal. In practice, this may mean that the actual purchase activity that can be observed based on transaction data is attributable to any given sub-goal, leaving the task of inferring the main goal to the retailer. In our fictitious scenario of Sally and Bob, for instance, the overall goal of the couple was to settle into their new home and neighborhood; sub-goals included decorating the house and garden, and organizing a large house-warming dinner for friends and neighbors. Doing all of this could conceivably involve a number of separate yet related trips to the store. The idea of the project-oriented consumer ticking off items on her materials list during each shopping trip is closely related to the concept of shopper "missions" (Sarantopoulos, Theotokis, Pramatari, & Doukidis, 2016), which emphasizes the shopper's need to complete concrete, purchase-related goals in a given trip.

In the retail context, a customer project broadly involves the procurement and assembly of a set of products to achieve a certain goal within a given timeframe. The size and complexity of the endeavor, and the sense of being "mission critical", are some criteria that we may use to distinguish projects from smaller tasks or chores.

Purchases related to a project may be completed over several shopping trips and across several stores (even at competing retailers), although this may be less of an issue if the customer wants to economize on her shopping time and could procure the project materials at a "one-stop shop" or "megastore" (Basker, Klimek, & Hoang Van, 2012; Messinger & Narasimhan, 1997). Projects may also be interrupted for a substantial duration of time and resumed at an unknown future time. For example, outdoor projects may be suspended during bad weather conditions. Other general issues, such as finding time to do the project in the face of multiple other deadlines or commitments, may also delay project completion. The resulting predictive problem for the retailer is similar to that faced by charities that encounter long pauses between successive gifts from a donor (Fader, Hardie, & Shang, 2010); the retailer may wrongly predict that a project has finished, when it is actually still in progress from the customer's perspective.

Moreover, the materials list related to a given project may span several product categories. In essence, the project-oriented customer is faced with a series of choice tasks in which she must process information on alternatives, and value cross-category product bundles (Russell et al., 1999). The subsequent decision to actually purchase a certain combination of project-related products may be based on the desire to maximize the perceived utility of the bundle. Retailers can implement bundling strategies when the rationale behind the product composition is clear and the utility of the bundle is similar for most customers. For instance, bundling a video gaming console with compatible video games, or a smartphone with a charger and earphones, makes sense as this allows customers to immediately start enjoying the bundle. In contrast, customer projects are complex and often situation-specific, making it difficult for the retailer to construct standard product bundles. Project-oriented customers are especially likely to prefer "solutions" encompassing the accurate fulfillment of the materials list and the provision of support services (e.g., assistance in assembling equipment) during project implementation (Tuli, Kohli, & Bharadwaj, 2007). In such a context, being able to predict customer projects could arguably help the retailer position itself as a solution provider.

Within the retail sector, the nature of customer projects may also differ based on whether the customer is another business (B2B) or an end-consumer (B2C). Project-related topics in the B2B setting include category management (Dhar, Hoch, & Kumar, 2001) and procurement planning (Bonser & Wu, 2001). The B2B customer may be another seller that wants to provide its own customers with an optimal assortment of products in the right store at the right time (Gruen & Shah, 2000). B2B customers can procure products in large batches over long purchase cycles (e.g., a new procurement order placed every month or season) and the batches may be similar over time. Meanwhile, B2C retailers face a customer base with fragmented buying patterns, in which projects can be more personal, smaller in scale, and more specifically defined. Knowing that customers are engaging in certain projects could impact the assortment planning of both B2B and B2C retailers (Mantrala et al., 2009). For example, retailers could deliberately make project-related products available in relevant store locations to influence the customer's store choice decision (Briesch, Chintagunta, & Fox, 2009), and cluster project-related items on particular aisles to take advantage of typical movement patterns of customers on the shop floor (Hui, Bradlow, & Fader, 2009; Hui, Fader, & Bradlow, 2009).

2.2 Predicting Customer Purchase Behavior and the Network Perspective

Since projects originate from customers, retailers can try predicting the customers' purchase behavior to meet project-based demand. Retailers are increasingly able to gather data on several aspects of their customer base, including transaction data, responses to ad campaigns, membership in loyalty programs, and activity on social media (Grewal et al., 2016). Although this paper focuses only on transaction data for simplicity of methodological exposition, the other forms of customer data mentioned above can arguably also be digitized and restructured as needed to enable a similar sort of database-driven analysis (Kotler, Keller, Manceau, & Hémonnet-Goujot, 2015; Rogers, 2005). Given the usefulness of knowing intentions in predicting actual behavior (Warshaw, 1980), retailers can use historical transaction data on a given customer as a signal of future purchases.

A key outcome of a predictive method in a retail setting may be a set of one or more products that can be recommended to a customer in the near future (e.g., the next shopping trip, or browsing session online). In this paper, we use methods based on best-seller lists and collaborative filtering as benchmarks for our network-based methods. The intuition for best-seller lists is captured by the so-called Recency, Frequency and Monetary (RFM) model (Fader, Hardie, & Lee, 2005). The model suggests that knowing how recently and frequently a customer purchased certain products, along with the associated monetary expenditure, can form the basis of future product recommendations. RFM models lend themselves to the implementation of "blockbuster strategies" (Elberse, 2008), in which "blockbuster" or best-selling products are recommended by default (or otherwise kept readily available in the store). These and other so-called "next product to buy" (NPTB) models can be used to cross-sell products between customers (Knott, Hayes, & Neslin, 2002). The notion of cross-selling is closely linked to that of project-based selling; in both cases, given that the customer has already bought a certain product, the retailer would like to sell additional (project-related) products that the customer may also be inclined to purchase (Li, Sun, & Montgomery, 2011). Typically, NPTB models score products based on their probability of being purchased by a customer. In practice, the top-scoring n products can then be recommended to the customer (e.g., on the first page of an online shop website). As such, what the exact size of n should be is a fundamental question in database marketing and generally depends on the empirical setting (Knott et al., 2002).

The intuition for collaborative filtering (CF) stems from the idea that, in order to increase the personalization and purchase probability of recommended products, predictive models can attempt to identify relationships between products. Two products may be related by being each other's complements or substitutes, being in related product categories, or being part of a project's materials list (Shocker, Bayus, & Kim, 2004). In a set-theoretic sense, related products may be thought of as being part of the same notional set, such as the set of products belonging to a customer project. CF is an increasingly popular method of deriving inter-product or inter-customer relationships (Sarwar, Karypis, Konstan, & Riedl, 2001). The success of CF rests on the central assumption that customers with similar purchase histories can be receptive to recommendations of similar products in the future. Crucially, approaches like CF take a network perspective of NPTB prediction by linking products in a co-purchase network. In particular, products can be represented as nodes in a network, where a link between any two products indicates that they have previously been purchased together. Past research has recognized the "network value" of products (Oestreicher-Singer, Libai, Sivan, Carmi, & Yassin, 2013), which broadly suggests that the economic value of a product is related to its position in the network. In particular, a product's value may partly be determined by neighboring products in the network. In the context of project-based marketing, a product that is closely linked to core items on the materials list is potentially also more likely to be purchased.

Note that, although the concepts from social network analysis (SNA) – centrality, density, and so on – can be used for product network analysis (PNA), the interpretation of these two types of networks is subtly different. In both cases, a tie between two nodes represents a relationship. However, people in social networks have agency and can form or remove social ties based on their preferences. A link in a social network can thus reflect similarity between the intrinsic properties of two people (e.g., liking something, or identifying with a group). By contrast, products do not inherently control their position in their network. As Dhar, Geva, Oestreicher-Singer, and Sundararajan (2014) explain, a link between two co-purchased products reflects the aggregate preferences of consumers that are necessarily not part of the product network. In other words, a strong tie between two products may suggest that several people bought both products in the same basket, but this can be independent of the product's intrinsic attributes (e.g., physical appearance or functionality). Since each link in a product network can capture several complex consumer preferences, networks allow us to take a parsimonious yet highly informative perspective on identifying project-based purchase behavior.

3. Methodology

3.1 Formalizing the Retailer's View of a Customer Project

As described in the previous section, customer projects can be conceptualized as complex, goal-oriented endeavors that may be constrained by resource availability and the customer's capabilities. From the retailer's perspective, projects essentially manifest themselves as a materials list or configuration of project-related products that can span across multiple categories and shopping trips, and may not necessarily all be purchased at the same store or even the same retailer (i.e., our so-called "focal retailer" from which we can obtain transaction data). Figure 1 gives a simplified, two-dimensional illustration of a customer project mapped onto the time and place of product purchases. The products purchased in the shaded region are not visible to the focal retailer.

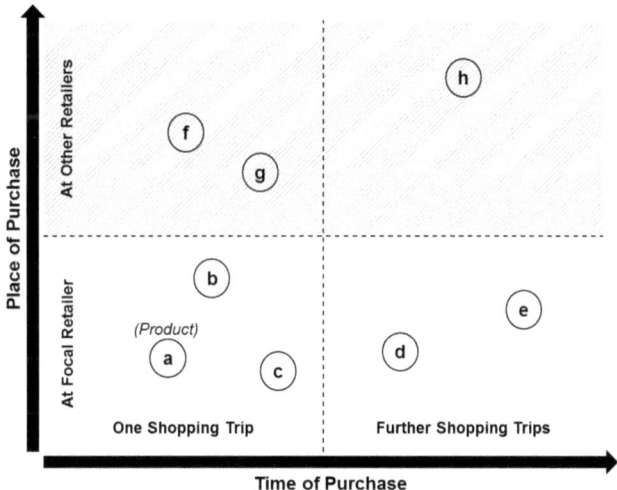

Figure 1: Two-Dimensional View of a Customer Project

25

The configurational view of projects can be formally captured by representing a project in terms of its materials list, namely as a set P of constituent products. The focal retailer only has visibility over some set P' of products purchased in its own stores, where P' is a subset of P. Thus the project shown in Figure 1 would be given by the set $P = \{a, b, c, d, e, f, g, h\}$, while the focal retailer's view would be $P' = \{a, b, c, d, e\}$. Depending on the store, the gap between P' and P can be problematic, e.g., if the focal store is a niche supplier of specific project components. For the datasets that we analyze in this paper, we can safely assume that $|P| \approx |P'|$, i.e., most of the purchases happen at the focal retailer. Also, notice that our specification of a project P abstracts away from the specific attributes of the constituent products (e.g., price and quantity), thereby keeping the focus on relationships between the products. As discussed next, the transaction data can now help us to approximately identify the project scope.

3.2 Specification of the Project Identification Problem

We assume that our retailer maintains the transaction data in a typical database table, where each row records the product purchased and each column stores an attribute of that product (e.g., timestamp, basket number, product ID, product information, and other store and customer details). Now we could try to slice this list of historically purchased products in such a way that each slice contains all products related to a given project. While there are other more complex forms of clustering that can be used to slice a customer's purchase history (Liao, 2005), we use a relatively simple slicing approach discussed below to keep the focus on the network-based aspect of our methodology in this paper.

In the simplest case, all project-related items would be purchased in a single shopping trip, so that the purchase history could be sliced by the corresponding shopping basket (or invoice number). In practice, such slicing may not always be straightforward. On the one hand, the slice may be too large, containing products that are unrelated to the corresponding project; this is problematic, since these extraneous products may wrongly be attributed to the same project and recommended in future project-based shopping trips. On the other hand, the slice may be too small, not fully capturing all project-related products. It is unclear whether a project prediction methodology should prefer smaller or larger slices in general, but we suggest that this issue can be mitigated by considering other contextual factors. For example, slicing by invoice number or shopping basket ID might make sense for B2B retailers whose customers follow a batch-oriented procurement pattern that maps more naturally onto individual shopping trips. Meanwhile, larger slices (in a temporal sense, e.g., days or weeks) may make sense for a B2C retailer whose customers engage in complex personal projects that are not be always fully thought-out at the outset; the larger slices thus allow for projects that could involve multiple trips to procure all materials. In general, we argue that conducting initial exploratory analyses of the given retail environment can help inform the choice of the most contextually meaningful slicing heuristic.

Having considered the above complications, let us suppose that a slice of the purchase history approximates the set of products belonging to a given project. Then the problem of project identification can be reframed as one of predicting set membership under information asymmetry. This problem can be formally constructed as follows. Suppose that a set P of products constitutes a project, but that one of the products, say y, is hidden. Then we (i.e., the retailer, or a predictive algorithm) have knowledge of the partial set $P_y = P - \{y\}$, as well as the list L_P of product purchases that occur prior to P. Now we can ask, does knowing (L_P, P_y) allow us to predict y? Or in a more relaxed formulation, does knowing (L_P, P_y) allow us to propose a set N of candidates for the hidden product, such that $y \in N$?

Note that the problem specification can be generalized to discover a set of multiple hidden products $Y = \{y_1, \ldots, y_k\}$, such that $P_Y = P - Y$; then we can ask whether knowing (L_P, P_Y) allows us to predict one or more of the members of the hidden set Y. Increasing the size of Y would presumably reduce the accuracy of the predictive algorithm. To see this intuitively, suppose that the probability of guessing a hidden product $y_i \in Y$ correctly is $\theta_i \in \Theta$, where Θ is the set of probabilities pertaining to the hidden products in Y, and let θ_{min} and θ_{max} denote the smallest and largest members of Θ, respectively. Then the lower and upper bounds for the expected probability of guessing at least one of the hidden products incorrectly are $1 - \theta_{max}^k$ and $1 - \theta_{min}^k$, respectively. However, the level of deterioration in predictive accuracy may vary depending on the size of k and the specific empirical context, neither of which fundamentally alters the development of our network-based methodology. Thus, for ease of exposition of our methodology, we only consider the case of a single hidden product y in this paper.

Now, as a solution to the above set membership problem, we could of course trivially propose a maximal set N_{max} that consists of all unique products that have already appeared in L_P, but this would not make sense in practice. A customer is only able to process information about a limited set of products at once, and a purchase decision in response to the proposed products may depend on other factors such as perceived variety (Kahn & Wansink, 2004). Moreover, although the optimal size of N may be different for every retailer and customer, past research suggests that N should not contain too many products, whether product consideration is happening offline or online (Kahn, Weingarten, & Townsend, 2013; Schmutz, Roth, Seckler, & Opwis, 2010). Based on this extant literature, we let $|N| \in [1,10]$ for the implementation of our predictive methodology.

The products we propose depend on our choice of method M to generate the candidate set N. In this paper we consider two network-based methods (using the concepts of tie strength and community structure, described in the next section), and two benchmark methods, namely the best-seller strategy (BS) and collaborative filtering (CF). We can evaluate the predictive performance of M by computing its hit-rate over several trials of randomly selected P_y from a holdout sample. Given the list L_P of historically purchased products, BS will always propose the best-selling products regardless of any information we obtain from P_y. As for CF, we will use an item-based implementation based on Sarwar et al. (2001). At the heart of item-based CF is an adjacency matrix A of products known from L_P, where an element A_{ij} gives the "similarity score" between products i and j; we use Pearson correlation as a measure of item-to-item similarity (Su & Khoshgoftaar, 2009). In sum, BS is the simpler and more naïve of the benchmarks, while CF is a close alternative to the network-based methods.

3.3 Operationalizing Product Network Analysis

Previous studies concerned with product network analysis (PNA) take different approaches to constructing the product network, but they all tend to implement variations on the idea of identifying co-occurrences between product pairs. In an online setting, for example, one could track the set of web pages linked to a focal product, or the e-commerce platform may provide co-purchasing information under a section typically titled "Users who bought this [the focal product] also bought [a list of other products]" (Dhar et al., 2014). More generally in offline and online settings, PNA can be seen as an extension of market basket analysis, such that we may consider all products occurring in a transaction (e.g., basket or invoice) to be "similar" or related in some sense (Kim, Kim, & Chen, 2012; Videla-Cavieres & Rios, 2014).

We follow this second approach, considering two products to be "similar" if they co-occur in that project. Intuitively, similarity by project membership would be represented by a tie between these products in a corresponding co-occurrence network. The operational steps of deriving a product network (or its representative adjacency matrix) from a raw transaction table can best be described via an example, as shown in Figure 2. This example assumes that slicing the purchase data by invoice number approximately splits the products into corresponding projects, although the process would hold for other slicing heuristics. Also note that the "handshaking problem" in Step 3 is a well-known counting problem that asks how many unique handshakes can occur in a room of n people; the solution is $\sum_{i=1}^{n-1} i$, corresponding to the number of ties generated by products in a given project.

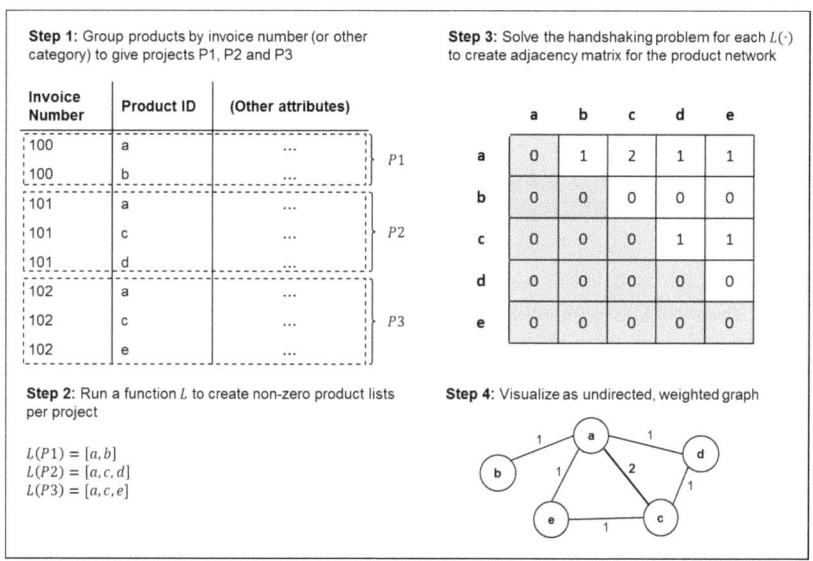

Figure 2: Derivation of a Product Network from Transaction Data

The notion of similarity in PNA can be understood at the micro-level (focusing on dyadic ties between products) or the macro-level (focusing on the community structure of the whole network, and the position of the focal node therein). We take the tie strength (TS) between any two products i and j to be a suitable micro-level measure of similarity, calling it $Sim_{TS}(i,j)$. In Figure 2, for example, $Sim_{TS}(a,b) = 1$ while $Sim_{TS}(a,c) = 2$, suggesting that a is more closely related to c (and therefore more likely to be in the same project). Note that we do not differentiate between in- and out-degrees since both imply co-occurrence in our methodology (Wasserman & Faust, 1994, pp. 93–101). At the macro-level, several community discovery methods exist to group nodes of a network (Coscia, Giannotti, & Pedreschi, 2011; Xie, Kelley, & Szymanski, 2013). Crucially, such analyses of the network structure can reveal clusters of project-related configurations of products. We opt for the implementation of modularity by Blondel, Guillaume,

Lambiotte, and Lefebvre (2008), which segments the nodes of the network into mutually exclusive groups (so-called "modularity classes"); see Appendix A1 for a formal definition of modularity. Essentially, any two products in a modularity class should co-occur more often than would be expected in a random graph. We can call this macro-level measure of similarity $Sim_{Mod}(i,j)$.

The set N of possible candidates for the hidden product y can be derived as follows. The neighborhood of y based on Sim_{TS} would be given by the set S_{TS} of all nodes θ in the set S of all nodes in the product network, such that $\forall \theta \in S: Sim_{TS}(y, \theta) > 0$. Meanwhile, the neighborhood of y based on Sim_{Mod} would be given by the set S_{Mod} of all nodes θ, such that $\forall \theta \in S: Sim_{Mod}(y, \theta) = 1$ (i.e., evaluates to "true") if y and θ are in the same modularity class. For both methods, we can define the nearest-neighbor set of a focal product i as S', such that $\forall y' \in S', y \in S: w(y') \geq w(y)$, where w is the weighted degree. While we use weighted degree to rank the nearest neighbors in this paper, other suitable ranking criteria may be derived from measures of betweenness or eigenvector centrality. Having ranked the nearest-neighbor products, we can propose a subset of products N with the highest w from the neighborhood as candidates for the hidden product y. The above discussion leads to the first two predictions of our research:

- **Prediction 1: Tie strength is a predictor of project composition**, i.e., there are likely to be enough dyadic ties between any two project-related products for Sim_{TS} to yield a statistically significant positive hit-rate.
- **Prediction 2: Modularity is a predictor of project composition**, i.e., any two project-related products are likely to be in the same modularity class often enough for Sim_{Mod} to yield a statistically significant positive hit-rate.

Note that, depending on the product network at hand, Sim_{TS} and Sim_{Mod} may lead us to different conclusions about project membership of any two products. Suppose we have a product z. If $z \in S'_{TS}$ but $z \notin S'_{Mod}$, then z can be thought of as being a "distant relative" of the hidden product y (i.e., z has a tie with y but is not in the same community). Conversely, if $z \in S'_{Mod}$ but $z \notin S'_{TS}$, then z is "weakly linked" to y (i.e., z has no direct tie with y but is in the same community). Interestingly, this suggests that the micro and macro level methods can be complementary to each other – if one method does not correctly map a given product to a project, the other method still might. In particular, we argue that this complementarity can be exploited by combining the proposal sets of both methods for guessing the hidden product y to increase the overall predictive accuracy. In line with previous literature on composite model-building (Blattberg & Hoch, 1990), we may expect an improvement in the predictive accuracy of a final proposal set of project-related products that includes the suggestions of different prediction methods. Thus we predict:

- **Prediction 3a: Tie strength and modularity are complementary predictors of project composition**, i.e., Sim_{TS} and Sim_{Mod} yield different hit patterns that do not fully overlap with each other.

Moreover, for certain retailers we may also find that the network methods complement those that we use as benchmarks (i.e., picking best-sellers, collaborative filtering). It is worth emphasizing that our motivation in this paper is not to pit the network-based methods against the benchmarks in an outright "horse race" in terms of hit-rates, since this will likely be of limited managerial value. The benchmark methods are relatively straightforward to grasp, implement and act upon in a practical retailing setting, and may perform quite well for highly skewed or long-established buying patterns. Thus, rather than positioning the network view as a complete alternative to the benchmark methods, we would argue that evidence of complementarity would make a strong business case for building the network methods on top of the more established benchmarks. This leads to the following prediction that we would like to test in our research:

- **Prediction 3b: The network-based methods and benchmarks are complementary predictors of project composition**, i.e., Sim_{TS} and Sim_{Mod} yield hit patterns that do not fully overlap with those of Sim_{BS} (best-seller) and Sim_{CF} (collaborative filtering), respectively.

4. Data

We implemented the network-based methodology and tested the related predictions on two separate retail datasets. In each case, the type of retailer, customer base and products are quite different, providing us with an opportunity to evaluate the external validity and generalizability of our methodology.

4.1 Online Gift Shop

The first dataset comes from a UK-based online gift shop and was originally obtained by Chen, Sain, and Guo (2012). The dataset covers a total of 538,993 transactions over a twelve-month period from December 2010 to December 2011. The following variables are recorded for each transaction: invoice number, invoice date, product ID, product name, quantity purchased, unit price (British pounds, i.e.,

GBP), customer ID, customer's country. The time and product variables are of particular interest to us with regard to the network-based methodology.

The merchandise encompasses gift items that may be appropriate for a range of occasions around the year. For example, the shop sells several holiday-themed items (e.g., decorations for Christmas), and other items oriented towards school-age children (e.g., backpacks and stationery). At the time of data collection, the shop does not have an offline presence and primarily caters to B2B customers. About 92% of the customers are based in the United Kingdom, and most of the remaining customers are in Europe. The top 1,000 customers in terms of purchase frequency are each responsible for more than 100 transactions in the dataset. The seasonal nature of the gift business is reflected in the clustering of several transactions around the Christmas shopping period (November to December), and to a lesser extent around the start and end of the UK summer holidays (July to September). Figure 3 summarizes the descriptive statistics of the gift shop dataset. The frequency distributions of customer and product IDs are both heavily skewed, although the latter has a thicker tail. These distributions, coupled with the fact that each invoice (or shopping trip) involves the purchase of about 274.83 units at 75.98 GBP reflect the planned stockpiling behavior of B2B customers (Chen et al., 2012). As such, we will slice the transaction data by invoice number for our project identification methodology.

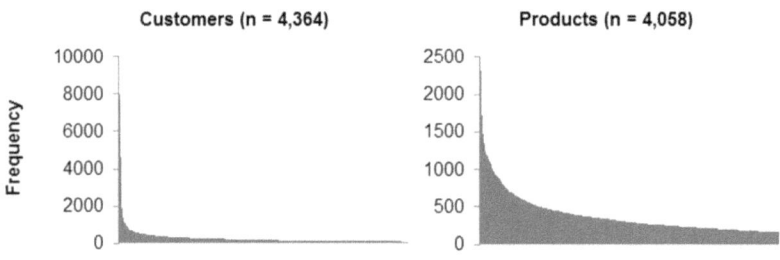

Sales summarized by invoice number:

	Min	Max	Mean	Std
Units	1.00	80995.00	274.83	947.88
Price (GBP)	0.03	5012.31	75.98	182.87

Figure 3: Descriptive Statistics of the Online Gift Shop Dataset

4.2 Local Grocery Store

The second dataset is from a Taiwanese grocery store, originally collected by Hsu, Chung, and Huang (2004). The dataset contains a total of 817,741 transactions over a four-month period from November 2000 to February 2001. The following variables are recorded for each transaction: transaction date, product ID, product class, quantity purchased, unit price (Taiwanese dollars, i.e., TWD), customer ID, customer's age, customer's residence area. Again, the time and product variables are of particular interest to us. Figure 4 shows the descriptive statistics for the data.

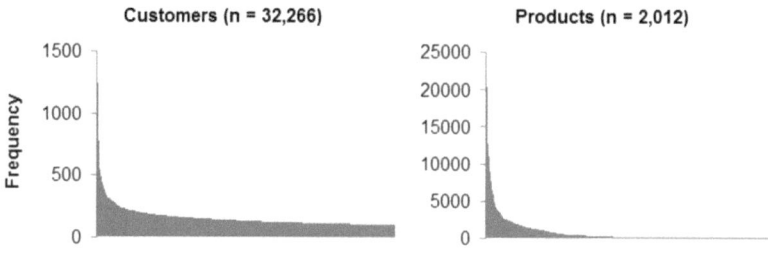

Sales summarized by month (1 GBP ≈ 48 TWD in the years 2000-2001):

	Min	Max	Mean	Std
Units	1.00	1,699.00	17.20	22.35
Price (TWD)	5.00	444,328.00	1641.50	3120.77

Figure 4: Descriptive Statistics of the Grocery Store Dataset

The grocery store sells food products as well as various small office supplies and furniture items. Like the previous gift shop data, the grocery store data shows skewed frequency distributions for customers and products. However, given its product assortment and its B2C customer base, we may expect any project-based purchases at the grocery store to be fragmented over multiple shopping trips. Indeed, based on the datasets, each shopping trip to the B2B gift shop involves the purchase of about 5 times as many products as a trip to the grocery store. On average fewer transactions occur per trip at the grocery store (17.2 units at 1,641.5 TWD). We also do not observe seasonality in the overall purchase pattern, as each month registers roughly 200,000 transactions. For the purposes of our empirical study, we will slice the transaction data by day, which may encompass multiple shopping trips. Lastly, although we do not make use of the customer age and residence details, it is interesting to note that about 70% of all purchases in the dataset are made by customer in the 35-50 year age group living in the two residence areas closest to the grocery store.

5. Results

5.1 Descriptive Network Statistics

Following the standard practice for evaluating the accuracy of models that predict future events like purchase behavior, we divide each dataset into a training and test sample (Knott et al., 2002). Given that the temporal order of observations is important in our context, we split the datasets timewise rather than generating a random holdout sample. Thus, we take the first 50% of transactions as the sample on which to train/calibrate our models, and the remainder serves as the holdout sample. For each of the retail dataset's training samples, we generate a network representation according to the methodology described previously in Section 3 using the programming language Python and the software Gephi (Bastian, Heymann, Jacomy, & others, 2009). A summary of the main network-level statistics is shown in Table 5.

Regarding the size of each network as seen from the number of nodes and edges, one might assume that since the gift shop data is larger than the grocery store data to begin with, the corresponding network of the training sample should also be larger. However, this need not necessarily be the case, since the variety of products purchased in each transaction also impacts the size of the network. For example, suppose that the transactions in the gift shop's training set did not include much product variety, i.e., all customers mainly bought the same small set of products. Then only those detected products would be available to form the network. The networks for the online gift shop and grocery store datasets capture about 91% and 95% of all products in the purchase history, respectively; this implies that the products missing from the network were evidently the sole item purchased in the corresponding shopping trip.

Network Statistics	B2B Online Gift Shop	B2C Grocery Store
Number of Nodes	3,694	1,913
Number of Edges	1,416,722	295,643
Average Degree	767.04	309.09
Graph Density	0.21	0.16
Network Diameter	3	4
Detected Communities	23	10

Table 5: Summary of Network-Level Descriptive Statistics by Dataset

Moreover, the statistics in Table 5 also suggest that the online shop network is generally denser than the other. The average degree of a network is given by the average number of edges incident on each node in the network. The online shop's product network, for instance, has an average degree of $2 * 1,416,722/3,694 = 767.04$. The network density measures how close the network is to being complete in a graph-theoretical sense. A complete network would include all possible edges between nodes and have a density of 1. Meanwhile, the network diameter is a measure of the longest distance between the any two nodes, where the distance between directly connected nodes is taken to be 1. A low diameter indicates a "small word" (Milgram, 1967). Taken together, we see that although both networks are fairly sparse, the gift shop network is denser and thus the corresponding products in the retail dataset co-occur more widely with each other. Lastly, we use the Louvain community detection algorithm by Blondel et al. (2008) that is implemented in Gephi to find that the gift shop network consists of about twice as many modularity classes as the grocery store network.

5.2 Performance of Network Methodology

5.2.1 Hit-Rates for Predictions of Project Composition

Having trained our benchmark and network-based methods, we compute hit-rates as follows. We begin by randomly selecting a slice P (approximating a project) from the holdout set. Recall that such a slice can encompass one or more shopping trips, depending on our choice of the slicing heuristic. As explained in Section 4, we slice the gift shop data by invoice, and the grocery store data by day. From each slice we randomly remove a product y, giving us a partial set P_y. To derive the proposal set N of candidates for y, we have four methods: the benchmarks best-seller (BS) and collaborative filtering (CF), and the network-based methods tie strength (TS) and modularity (Mod). Note that we can vary the size of the proposal set. Let N_M be the proposal set for a method $M \in \{BS, CF, TS, Mod\}$. Then we can compute a hit-rate sample $Hits_M(y, P_y, N_M, n)$ of size n for each combination of hidden product y, partial set P_y and predictions N_M. This setup allows us to analyze the case of $P_y = P - \{y\}$ (proposing related products, i.e., whether knowing other project-related products lets us predict y).

The above setup allows us to directly test Predictions 1 and 2, namely that tie strength and community structure (modularity) are significant predictors of project composition. To this end, Table 6 presents the results of the project prediction methods for various $|N_M|$ over $n = 1,000$ trials. Table 6 allows us to visually check the robustness of the predictive methods across the two datasets over different proposal set sizes. Sample averages (μ_M) of $Hits_M$ are shown with standard errors in brackets. The statistical significance of each hit-rate result is obtained via a one-sample test of proportion of the null hypothesis $H_0: \mu_M = 0$.

The results largely support Predictions 1 and 2, since both tie strength and community structure are generally statistically significant predictors of project composition, often at the 1% significance level. While the hit-rates may seem small, they can actually be quite large in absolute terms in practice, where a typical retailer (especially online stores) might execute several million transactions in a short space of time. The hit-rates of the network-based methods are of a comparable order of magnitude to those of the benchmark methods, although the actual values of the hit-rates are heavily dependent on the particular dataset and implementation of the respective methods. For example, in the case of the online gift shop data, tie strength tends to outperform the remaining three methods. For the grocery store data, both network-based methods outperform CF.

$|N_M|$:	B2B Online Gift Shop		B2C Grocery Store	
	μ_{TS}	μ_{Mod}	μ_{TS}	μ_{Mod}
1	0.007 (0.003)***	0.001 (0.001)	0.008 (0.003)***	0.015 (0.004)***
3	0.015 (0.004)***	0.003 (0.002)*	0.024 (0.005)***	0.020 0.004)***
5	0.021 (0.005)***	0.004 (0.002)**	0.037 (0.006)***	0.034 (0.006)***
10	0.034 (0.006)***	0.005 (0.002)**	0.058 (0.007)***	0.056 (0.007)***
$|N_M|$:	μ_{BS}	μ_{CF}	μ_{BS}	μ_{CF}
1	0.004 (0.063)**	0.000 (0.000)	0.017 (0.129)***	0.000 (0.000)
3	0.012 (0.109)***	0.006 (0.077)**	0.036 (0.186)***	0.004 (0.063)**
5	0.017 (0.129)***	0.007 (0.083)***	0.056 (0.230)***	0.007 (0.083)***
10	0.034 (0.181)***	0.016 (0.126)***	0.120 (0.325)***	0.021 (0.143)***
*** p<0.01, ** p<0.05, * p<0.1				

Table 6: Hit-Rates of Project Prediction Methods

The hit-rates of the network-based methods are also better that the corresponding expectations of a random draw from the set of all (unique) products in the respective datasets. To see this analytically, suppose we obtain a set S of all products that appear in the historical purchase data. Then given some required size $|N_M|$ of the proposal set, basic combinatorics would lead us to expect a hit-rate of $\frac{(|N_M|)!(|S|-|N_M|)!}{(|S|)!}$ for a random draw of $|N_M|$ proposed products from the full product set S. Since $|S|$ is much larger than $|N_M|$ in our empirical setup, this expected hit-rate will be vanishingly small. For example, considering the online gift shop data for $|N_M| = 1$ shown in Table 6, the expected hit-rate of a random draw would be $\frac{1}{4058} \approx 0.02\%$ (where 4058 is the total number of unique products, as shown in Figure 3), which is several times smaller than the corresponding hit-rates of the network methodologies. It is interesting to note that, while the hit-rates of the network-methods appear to improve as $|N_M|$ increases (see Table 6), the hit-rates of the corresponding random draws are expected to drop as $(|N_M|)! \, (|S| - |N_M|)!$ grows more slowly than $(|S|)!$ with each increase in $|N_M|$; this intuitively reflects the value of the information gained from the network analysis.

Mean Comparisons	B2B Online Gift Shop		B2B Online Gift Shop	
	Popular Products	Long-Tail Products	Popular Products	Long-Tail Products
$\mu_{TS} - \mu_{BS}$	-0.125 (0.011)***	0.040 (0.003)***	-0.153 (0.007)***	0.030 (0.003)***
$\mu_{TS} - \mu_{CF}$	0.064 (0.007)***	0.021 (0.003)***	0.079 (0.005)***	0.010 (0.003)***
$\mu_{TS} - \mu_{Mod}$	0.074 (0.007)***	0.036 (0.003)***	-0.006 (0.005)	0.019 (0.003)***
$\mu_{Mod} - \mu_{BS}$	-0.199 (0.010)***	0.005 (0.001)***	-0.147 (0.006)***	0.010 (0.002)***
$\mu_{Mod} - \mu_{CF}$	-0.010 (0.004)***	-0.014 (0.002)***	0.085 (0.005)***	-0.009 (0.003)***
$\mu_{BS} - \mu_{CF}$	0.189 (0.010)***	-0.019 (0.002)***	0.232 (0.006)***	-0.019 (0.002)***
*** $p<0.01$, ** $p<0.05$, * $p<0.1$, n = 10000				

Table 7: Comparing Performances of Methods for Long-Tail Products

We also test whether the performance of each method is different based on the characteristics of the hidden product y (e.g., its best-seller rank and frequency of purchase). In particular, it would be of theoretical and practical interest to compare the performances of the four methods for popular products and long-tail products. One approach to investigate this is to rank the products in descending order of popularity based on the purchase history. Then all products with a rank below some threshold τ can be considered the popular ones, and the rest can be the long-tail products. Letting $\tau = 100$, Table 7 gives the results of paired two-sample tests of proportions on a sample of 10,000 trials comparing the performances of the network-based and benchmark methods with respect to product popularity.

The best-seller method evidently does better that the others for popular products, while the results for the CF method are mixed. Arguably the more interesting observation in this analysis, however, is that tie strength outperforms the remaining methods for long-tail products in both datasets, guessing up to 400 more hidden products correctly. As such, Table 7 adds nuance to the hit-rates shown earlier in Table 6, since it suggests that the strong performance of the best-seller method (and to some extent that of CF) is mainly driven by the popular products. Why does tie strength outperform the other methods? The short answer is that this depends on our implementations of the methods. In our setup, best-seller lists by definition only propose one or more of the top 10 products seen in the purchase history, so it is trivial to show that this benchmark method will never correctly guess any of the remaining products. The analysis done by Fleder and Hosanagar (2009) suggests that the item-based CF method we use may also be somewhat popularity-biased, although to a lesser extent than best-seller lists. Lastly, the implementation by Blondel et al. (2008) yields modularity classes with an average of about 161 and 191 products per class for the gift shop and grocery store datasets, respectively (see Table 5). Depending on the specification of the proposal set size, one or more of the top 10 products with the highest degree are proposed as candidates for the hidden product. Since the degree measure is a reflection of popularity, the modularity method is also somewhat popularity-biased. Although the tie strength method also proposes nearest-neighbor products with the highest degrees, the nearest-neighbor sets themselves are much smaller than the modularity classes, thus mitigating the effect of popularity.

5.2.2 Complementarity of Predictive Methods

In the context of the hit-rate samples $Hits_M$ generated for each method M, we can formulate the setup for the complementarity analysis as follows. Suppose we wish to combine predictive strengths of the micro and macro network methods to propose a candidate set of size η. Then, without assuming any additional information about TS and Mod, we could simply take the top $\eta/2$ candidates from each of their proposal sets, and build a combined set of size η out of these. Now to establish the presence of complementarity, we can derive a hit-rate sample $Hits_{TS \oplus Mod}$ from the exclusive union (i.e., the XOR function) of $Hits_{TS}$ and $Hits_{Mod}$. Crucially, $Hits_{TS \oplus Mod}$ yields a hit when only one of either $Hits_{TS}$ or $Hits_{Mod}$ does so; this captures the notion that two methods are complementary if their combined hit-rate is larger than their separate hit-rates (i.e., the methods compensate for each other's weaknesses). To see whether the two methods combined produce a higher predictive accuracy than each method on its own, we can test $H_0: \mu_{TS \oplus Mod} \leq 0$ with a one-sample test of proportion.

Based on the samples presented in Table 6, we can demonstrate the intuitive procedure for checking complementarity fairly elegantly with the following numerical example. Suppose we wish to build a combined network-based proposal set of size 10 to predict related products. Then with our above reasoning, we would like to jointly propose the top 5 candidates from each of the corresponding network-based proposal sets N_{TS} and N_{Mod}, which is equivalent to simply picking the full sets we generated for $|N_M| = 5$. Now an analysis of the union of their hit-rate samples shows that, out of the 1,000 trials, never once did both methods make the correct prediction; the tie strength method was correct 21 times and the modularity method was correct 4 times, but there was no overlap in these hits. Therefore, the combined proposal set would beat the better of the two individual methods (namely tie strength) by $1 - \frac{21+4}{21} \approx 19\%$ in terms of predictive accuracy.

The above setup lets us test Prediction 3a (that tie strength and community structure are complementary), and can be reused with a small modification to test Prediction 3b (comparing network methods with benchmarks). In particular, the $\oplus$ operator in $Hits_{X \oplus Y}$ treats both methods X and Y as "equals", i.e., neither is necessarily the default or preferred method of a given retailer ex-ante. By contrast, a retailer would presumably already be using one the methods we consider as benchmarks (or some variation on those), and may be reluctant to abandon the existing method outright. In this sense, a new (network-based) method is realistically only deemed to be complementary if it improves the hit-rate beyond that of the existing method. We therefore define a new union-type operator, say $\ominus$, to combine hit-rate samples such that $Hits_{X \ominus Y}$ records a hit only when X has a hit and Y does not. For example, consider a scenario in which a benchmark method Y "overshadows" a network-based method X completely, i.e., for every hit that X achieves, Y also records a hit. If Y records more hits than X, then $Hits_{X \oplus Y}$ may end up with a sample mean significantly above zero, but this would be driven purely by the strong performance of the benchmark method Y. In contrast, the sample mean of $Hits_{X \ominus Y}$ would only be greater than zero when the network-based method X performs better, and thus gives the retailer reason to consider combining the benchmark and network methods. Table 8 shows the results of the complementarity analysis (at $|N_M| = 5$ to aid understanding). Given a combined hit-rate sample X$\oplus$Y (or X $\ominus$ Y, as the case may be) of methods X and Y over 1000 trials, we run a one-sample test of proportion of the null hypothesis $H_0: \mu_{X \oplus Y} = 0$.

The results support Predictions 3a/b, suggesting that the network-based methods are complementary predictors with respect to each other as well as the benchmarks. Combining tie strength and modularity leads to statistically significant improvements in predictive accuracy of up to 0.53%. Similarly, combining the network-based methods with the benchmark methods can lead to improvements of up to 0.36%. To put this into perspective, the combined methods could yield several thousand additional hits daily for a typical e-retailer at the time of writing.

Combination at $|N_M| = 5$	B2B Online Gift Shop	B2C Grocery Store
$TS \oplus Mod$	0.025 (0.005)***	0.053 (0.007)***
$TS \ominus BS$	0.018 (0.004)***	0.028 (0.005)***
$TS \ominus CF$	0.019 (0.004)***	0.036 (0.006)***
$Mod \ominus BS$	0.004 (0.002)**	0.013 (0.004)***
$Mod \ominus CF$	0.003 (0.002)**	0.034 (0.006)***
*** p<0.01, ** p<0.05, * p<0.1, n = 1000		

Table 8: Complementarity of Network-Based Methods per Dataset

5.2.3 Convergence Properties of Predictive Accuracy

The empirical setup also allows us to analyze how the predictive performance of each method changes in response to increased information and relaxed constraints. We would intuitively expect predictive accuracies to initially improve, but then begin to plateau as the power of each predictive method is exhausted. Specifically, we can track predictions for different sizes of P (project sets) and N_M (candidate proposal sets). We would expect larger project sets to correlate positively with performance in the case of predicting related products, due to the greater information content of $P_y = P - \{y\}$. We would also generally expect larger proposal sets to lead to better hit-rates, simply because of the increased probability of y being in N_M.

Correlation analyses of the hit-rates match our expectations, but it is interesting to note that the correlation with project set size is generally small (less than 0.01). Intuitively, we can see this by considering a hypothetical small project $P1 = \{x, y, z\}$ and a larger project $P2 = \{u, v, w, x, y, z\}$. In each case we hide y and try to predict it with our various methods. Suppose we wish to build a candidate proposal set of some size η. The best-seller method does not make use of P_y, so there is no correlation with project size by definition. The remaining three methods all essentially build the proposal sets by picking the top η/k candidates from each of the k products in P_y (i.e., the neighboring products). Notice that since η is fixed, η/k increases as the project size k decreases (i.e., each neighbor provides a larger

40

list of candidates). If the neighbors are well-connected in the network, which appears to be the case for our data as seen from the network density statistics in Table 5, then offering enough candidates should not be a problem for large η/k; this is especially the case since we have capped η at 10, and k is at least 1. Thus, the low correlation is observed because the overall information available to the predictive method does not necessarily decrease with smaller project sizes in our problem specification, which is based on practical considerations.

Finally, we can analyze how the variation in historically observed products converges with each transaction in the purchase data. The transactions of variety-seeking customers would reveal several more products to our co-occurrence analysis than those of more monotonous customers. After how many observed transactions will we have seen all product co-occurrences in the retailer's assortment? Note that, in an assortment of y products, at most $y * (y - 1)$ pairs can be discovered, each of which will be captured in the co-occurrence matrices used in our network-based methodology. Thus, to answer the above question, we track the saturation of the co-occurrence matrices with each new observed transaction. We find that the matrices are very sparse and thus any new product observed generally represents a new co-occurrence. For example, we only discover 21.6%, and 11.6% of all possible product pairs in the gift shop and grocery store datasets respectively. With enough transactions we would logically expect the matrix to become saturated, such that the next observed product co-occurrence is no longer a new one. Crucially, analyzing the saturation of co-occurrence matrices over time may let us infer latent buying strategies of project-oriented customers. For instance, a low saturation rate may indicate a highly planned and repetitive buying strategy (e.g., as in the case of seasonal projects), while high saturation rates may indicate the opposite (e.g., shorter, more varied projects).

6. Discussion and Conclusion

Project-based buying as a concept has received little explicit attention in marketing literature so far, although its relevance to understanding consumer behavior has been suggested before (Gao, Huang, & Simonson, 2014; Russell et al., 1999). The overarching aim of this paper is to advance a network perspective of project-based purchase behavior. We therefore begin by presenting a theoretically grounded, network-based understanding of project-based buying as a complex, goal-oriented endeavor (Bagozzi & Dholakia, 1999; Grewal et al., 2016). Building on this foundation, the paper makes two main contributions to marketing research. Firstly, we tackle the problem of identifying projects based on customer purchase histories by formalizing it as an empirically testable problem of predicting set membership. In particular, we conceptualize projects in terms of a network of co-purchased products that derive utility for the customer by being part of a particular project. We use measures from micro- and macro-level product network analysis, extending previous empirical work on co-occurrence networks (Dhar et al., 2014; Oestreicher-Singer et al., 2013). Secondly, we test the network-based methods on the datasets of two different retailers to find that both tie strength and community are significant and complementary predictors of project composition. The network-based methods can also be combined with predictive benchmarks such as the best-seller strategy and collaborative filtering to derive improvements in the resulting predictive accuracy. Our empirical setup also facilitates the analysis of some interesting convergence properties of predictive accuracy.

The work presented in this paper leads to some interesting theoretical implications for model-building efforts related to the prediction of consumer behavior in the retail setting. In line with the observations of Lilien and Rangaswamy (2000), our work highlights the value of taking a network perspective in building models for marketing decisions. While we mainly analyze the effectiveness of network measures in building purchase prediction models (Knott et al., 2002), other areas of marketing theory (e.g., store layout planning, assortment and procurement planning) may benefit from considering the value of connections between products. The underlying idea which can be leveraged across all these areas of application is that seemingly unrelated entities (e.g., items from different product categories) may be related by way of membership in some latent group, and these latent relationships can be uncovered using network analysis. Moreover, we show the usefulness of combining results obtained from different methods (e.g., product recommendations by network-based and other baseline measures) in deriving more accurate predictions; this echoes the views of Blattberg and Hoch (1990), that it may be worthwhile to build composite models to improve predictive performance. In general, our approach to analyzing the complementarities and convergence properties of the network methodology also represents a theoretically valuable alternative to the dominant hypothesis approach that pervades much of empirical work in marketing science (Brodie & Danaher, 2000).

Our empirical methodology and results have both strategic and operational implications for retail marketers across online and offline channels. At a strategic level, this paper arguably makes a valid case for incorporating network-based measures in the evaluation of – and response to – customer behavior. In particular, while retailers have already begun to pay attention to "people networks" via social media marketing, we would argue that more attention should also be given to "product networks" in terms of the analysis of product co-occurrence patterns. These network-based insights can allow the development of a customer-centric marketing strategy, for B2C as well as B2B customer bases (Tuli et al., 2007). Especially for retailers that receive high customer traffic, every small gain in predictive accuracy created by network analysis can potentially boost the bottom line. At an operational level, a retailer wanting to implement the network perspective can use the computational methodology outlined in this paper as a template. Our method is scalable for large product assortments and offers a number of options for customization (e.g., size of proposal sets, project sets and depth of product histories). Perhaps equally importantly, our method is essentially modular in its specification and can be integrated with the customer analytics infrastructure that the retailer may already be deploying. After all, the network method relies on the same underlying transactional databases, and can therefore be added as a custom module into the existing analytics software.

Future work can look at addressing the two main limitations of our current approach, namely the assumptions made in our problem specification and the challenge of generalizing our empirical findings. For instance, we make some key assumptions about customer behavior to enable convenient heuristics for slicing purchase histories (e.g., assuming the occurrence of repeat purchases and that most of these happen at the focal store). Despite having obtained encouraging results from two datasets, contextual differences make it inherently difficult to confirm the external validity of our findings. Thus, future work can attempt to formalize the project identification problem under more relaxed assumptions and test it using additional data. Moreover, our research can also be extended in novel directions. In addition to considering more network-based measures, we could investigate project-based buying behavior across different store locations of the same retailer. For example, Pennacchioli, Coscia, Rinzivillo, Pedreschi, and Giannotti (2013) analyze distance-related range effects, and one could conceivably look at this from a network perspective. Overall, the theoretical and practical insights that emerge from our research highlight the fruitfulness of studying project-based buying through the lens of product networks. The network-based perspective on the project identification problem allows us to benefit from past work in a number of different research areas, such as retailing and marketing science (Mantrala et al., 2009; Natter, Reutterer, Mild, & Taudes, 2007; Russell & Petersen, 2000), information systems (Dhar et al., 2014) and computational science (Coscia et al., 2011; Xie et al., 2013). We ultimately hope that our paper will encourage others to take a network perspective of customer behavior as part of their future research agenda.

Appendix

A1. Formal Definition of Modularity Measure

We describe the formalization in terms of a network $G = (V, E)$ with $|V|$ nodes and $|E|$ edges. The network can equally be described by a weighted matrix W, such that the element W_{ij} represents the strength of the edge between nodes i and j (e.g., frequency of co-occurrences in the case of event data). Let the adjacency matrix A_{ij} denote a non-weighted version of W_{ij}, such that the element $A_{ij} = 1$ if nodes i and j are connected and 0 otherwise. Then the typical definition of the modularity class c of node i is derived as follows (Newman, 2010; Wasserman & Faust, 1994). The modularity of a network partition is given by $Q = \frac{1}{2m} \Sigma_{i,j} \left[W_{ij} - \frac{k_i k_j}{2m} \right] \delta(c_i, c_j)$, where $k_i = \Sigma_j W_{ij}$, c_i is the modularity class (or network community/cluster) to which node i is assigned, $\delta(c_i, c_j) = 1$ if $c_i = c_j$ and 0 otherwise, and $m = \frac{1}{2} \Sigma_{ij} W_{ij}$.

References

Bagozzi, R. P., & Dholakia, U. (1999). Goal setting and goal striving in consumer behavior. *Journal of Marketing,* 19–32.

Basker, E., Klimek, S., & Hoang Van, P. (2012). Supersize It: The Growth of Retail Chains and the Rise of the "Big-Box" Store. *Journal of Economics & Management Strategy, 21*(3), 541–582.

Bastian, M., Heymann, S., Jacomy, M., & others. (2009). Gephi: an open source software for exploring and manipulating networks. *ICWSM, 8,* 361–362.

Blattberg, R. C., & Hoch, S. J. (1990). Database models and managerial intuition: 50% model+ 50% manager. *Management Science, 36*(8), 887–899.

Blondel, V. D., Guillaume, J.-L., Lambiotte, R., & Lefebvre, E. (2008). Fast unfolding of communities in large networks. *Journal of Statistical Mechanics: Theory and Experiment, 2008*(10), P10008.

Bodapati, A. V. (2008). Recommendation systems with purchase data. *Journal of Marketing Research, 45*(1), 77–93.

Bonser, J. S., & Wu, S. D. (2001). Procurement planning to maintain both short-term adaptiveness and long-term perspective. *Management Science, 47*(6), 769–786.

Briesch, R. A., Chintagunta, P. K., & Fox, E. J. (2009). How does assortment affect grocery store choice? *Journal of Marketing Research, 46*(2), 176–189.

Brodie, R. J., & Danaher, P. J. (2000). Building models for marketing decisions: Improving empirical procedures. *International Journal of Research in Marketing, 17*(2), 135–139.

Chen, D., Sain, S. L., & Guo, K. (2012). Data mining for the online retail industry: A case study of RFM model-based customer segmentation using data mining. *Journal of Database Marketing & Customer Strategy Management, 19*(3), 197–208.

Coscia, M., Giannotti, F., & Pedreschi, D. (2011). A classification for community discovery methods in complex networks. *Statistical Analysis and Data Mining, 4*(5), 512–546.

Dhar, S. K., Hoch, S. J., & Kumar, N. (2001). Effective category management depends on the role of the category. *Journal of Retailing, 77*(2), 165–184.

Dhar, V., Geva, T., Oestreicher-Singer, G., & Sundararajan, A. (2014). Prediction in economic networks. *Information Systems Research, 25*(2), 264–284.

Elberse, A. (2008). Should you invest in the long tail? *Harvard Business Review, 86*(7/8), 88.

Fader, P. S., Hardie, B. G. S., & Lee, K. L. (2005). RFM and CLV: Using iso-value curves for customer base analysis. *Journal of Marketing Research, 42*(4), 415–430.

Fader, P. S., Hardie, B. G. S., & Shang, J. (2010). Customer-base analysis in a discrete-time noncontractual setting. *Marketing Science, 29*(6), 1086–1108.

Fleder, D., & Hosanagar, K. (2009). Blockbuster culture's next rise or fall: The impact of recommender systems on sales diversity. *Management Science, 55*(5), 697–712.

Gao, L., Huang, Y., & Simonson, I. (2014). The Influence of Initial Possession Level on Consumers' Adoption of a Collection Goal: A Tipping Point Effect. *Journal of Marketing, 78*(6), 143–156.

Goldenberg, B. J. (2008). *CRM in Real Time: Empowering Customer Relationships.* Medford, NJ: CyberAge Books.

Grewal, D., Roggeveen, A. L., & Nordfält, J. (2016). Roles of retailer tactics and customer-specific factors in shopper marketing: Substantive, methodological, and conceptual issues. *Journal of Business Research, 69*(3), 1009–1013.

Gruen, T. W., & Shah, R. H. (2000). Determinants and outcomes of plan objectivity and implementation in category management relationships. *Journal of Retailing, 76*(4), 483–510.

Hsu, C.-N., Chung, H.-H., & Huang, H.-S. (2004). Mining skewed and sparse transaction data for personalized shopping recommendation. *Machine Learning, 57*(1-2), 35–59.

Hui, S. K., Bradlow, E. T., & Fader, P. S. (2009). Testing behavioral hypotheses using an integrated model of grocery store shopping path and purchase behavior. *Journal of Consumer Research, 36*(3), 478–493.

Hui, S. K., Fader, P. S., & Bradlow, E. T. (2009). Path data in marketing: An integrative framework and prospectus for model building. *Marketing Science, 28*(2), 320–335.

Kahn, B. E., & Wansink, B. (2004). The influence of assortment structure on perceived variety and consumption quantities. *Journal of Consumer Research, 30*(4), 519–533.

Kahn, B. E., Weingarten, E., & Townsend, C. (2013). Assortment variety: too much of a good thing. *Review of Marketing Research, 10*(1), 1–23.

Kim, H. K., Kim, J. K., & Chen, Q. Y. (2012). A product network analysis for extending the market basket analysis. *Expert Systems with Applications, 39*(8), 7403–7410.

Knott, A., Hayes, A., & Neslin, S. A. (2002). Next-product-to-buy models for cross-selling applications. *Journal of Interactive Marketing, 16*(3), 59–75.

Kotler, P., Keller, K. L., Manceau, D., & Hémonnet-Goujot, A. (2015). *Marketing Management* (Vol. 14). Englewood Cliffs, NJ: Prentice Hall.

Li, S., Sun, B., & Montgomery, A. L. (2011). Cross-selling the right product to the right customer at the right time. *Journal of Marketing Research, 48*(4), 683–700.

Liao, T. W. (2005). Clustering of time series data - a survey. *Pattern Recognition, 38*(11), 1857–1874.

Lilien, G. L., & Rangaswamy, A. (2000). Modeled to bits: Decision models for the digital, networked economy. *International Journal of Research in Marketing, 17*(2), 227–235.

Mantrala, M. K., Levy, M., Kahn, B. E., Fox, E. J., Gaidarev, P., Dankworth, B., & Shah, D. (2009). Why is assortment planning so difficult for retailers? A framework and research agenda. *Journal of Retailing, 85*(1), 71–83.

Messinger, P. R., & Narasimhan, C. (1997). A model of retail formats based on consumers' economizing on shopping time. *Marketing Science, 16*(1), 1–23.

Milgram, S. (1967). The small world problem. *Psychology Today, 2*(1), 60–67.

Natter, M., Reutterer, T., Mild, A., & Taudes, A. (2007). Practice Prize Report-An Assortmentwide Decision-Support System for Dynamic Pricing and Promotion Planning in DIY Retailing. *Marketing Science, 26*(4), 576–583.

Newman, M. (2010). *Networks: An introduction*: Oxford University Press.

Ngai, E. W. T., Xiu, L., & Chau, D. C. K. (2009). Application of data mining techniques in customer relationship management: A literature review and classification. *Expert Systems with Applications, 36*(2), 2592–2602.

Oestreicher-Singer, G., Libai, B., Sivan, L., Carmi, E., & Yassin, O. (2013). The network value of products. *Journal of Marketing, 77*(3), 1–14.

Pennacchioli, D., Coscia, M., Rinzivillo, S., Pedreschi, D., & Giannotti, F. (2013). Explaining the product range effect in purchase data. In *IEEE International Conference on Big Data* (pp. 648–656).

Rogers, M. (2005). Customer strategy: Observations from the trenches. *Journal of Marketing, 69*(4), 262–263.

Russell, G. J., & Petersen, A. (2000). Analysis of cross category dependence in market basket selection. *Journal of Retailing, 76*(3), 367–392.

Russell, G. J., Ratneshwar, S., Shocker, A. D., Bell, D., Bodapati, A., Degeratu, A., . . . Shankar, V. H. (1999). Multiple-category decision-making: Review and synthesis. *Marketing Letters, 10*(3), 319–332.

Sarantopoulos, P., Theotokis, A., Pramatari, K., & Doukidis, G. (2016). Shopping missions: An analytical method for the identification of shopper need states. *Journal of Business Research, 69*(3), 1043–1052.

Sarwar, B., Karypis, G., Konstan, J., & Riedl, J. (2001). Item-based collaborative filtering recommendation algorithms. In *Proceedings of the 10th International Conference on World Wide Web* (pp. 285–295).

Schmutz, P., Roth, S. P., Seckler, M., & Opwis, K. (2010). Designing product listing pages—Effects on sales and users' cognitive workload. *International Journal of Human-Computer Studies, 68*(7), 423–431.

Shocker, A. D., Bayus, B. L., & Kim, N. (2004). Product complements and substitutes in the real world: The relevance of "other products". *Journal of Marketing, 68*(1), 28–40.

Su, X., & Khoshgoftaar, T. M. (2009). A survey of collaborative filtering techniques. *Advances in Artificial Intelligence, 2009,* 4.

Tuli, K. R., Kohli, A. K., & Bharadwaj, S. G. (2007). Rethinking customer solutions: From product bundles to relational processes. *Journal of Marketing, 71*(3), 1–17.

Videla-Cavieres, I. F., & Rios, S. A. (2014). Extending market basket analysis with graph mining techniques: A real case. *Expert Systems with Applications, 41*(4), 1928–1936.

Warshaw, P. R. (1980). Predicting purchase and other behaviors from general and contextually specific intentions. *Journal of Marketing Research,* 26–33.

Wasserman, S., & Faust, K. (1994). *Social network analysis: Methods and applications* (Vol. 8): Cambridge University Press.

Xie, J., Kelley, S., & Szymanski, B. K. (2013). Overlapping community detection in networks: The state-of-the-art and comparative study. *ACM Computing Surveys, 45*(4), 43.

Essay 2:

The DNA of Winning Ideas - A Network Perspective of Success in New Product Development

Chinmay Kakatkar, Julia de Groote, Johann Füller and Martin Spann

Abstract

The identification of potentially successful ideas is a key challenge for scholars and practitioners of innovation, especially in the context of new product development. Extant literature suggests that the composition of the idea itself may play an important role in explaining the success of the idea. However, there has been a relative paucity of innovation and marketing research investigating the nature of the idea further. We address this gap with two main contributions. First, we develop a configurational theory about the idea itself (i.e., the "idea DNA"), which suggests that an idea's compositional features and their configuration may be strong predictors of success. Second, we develop a new network-based methodology that aims at extracting the DNA of successful ideas, thereby providing the opportunity of identifying further promising ideas in a given domain. We validate this methodology using a dataset from an idea competition in the consumer goods sector. The evidence suggests that an idea's features and meta-features derived from network analysis can be strong predictors of success. Our methodology lends itself to practical adoption by managers to improve existing innovation processes.

Keywords: Idea Selection, Ingredient Networks, Idea Templates, Text Mining, Machine Learning, Idea Competitions, Crowdsourcing

1. Introduction

When A. G. Lafley became CEO of Procter & Gamble in 2000, the consumer goods company was in troubled times. A key problem was that, as a mature business, P&G had seemingly forgotten how to innovate. The percentage of new products that were deemed commercially viable had leveled off at 35%, and just 15% of all P&G innovations were meeting their financial targets (Brown & Anthony, 2011; Huston & Sakkab, 2006). When Lafley took the reins, he placed innovation at the heart of his turnaround strategy, challenging the staff to rethink their approach to identifying and developing promising new ideas. He held that successful ideas could come from anywhere, both within the firm and beyond, and could result from innovative combinations of the old and the new. Recognizing successful ideas as early and cost-effectively as possible was especially important, as this would allow P&G to better allocate its resources and give more time to nurture the ideas to success (Lafley & Charan, 2008).

As the above example highlights, the identification of "winning" ideas is a central issue in innovation research and practice. Ideas are typically considered innovative by an adopter if they are perceived as being novel, challenging the present order in some sense (Rogers, 2003). For instance, such innovativeness may arise from new discoveries, the invention of a new mechanism, or a new combination of existing ideas. In order to remain competitive, firms could in theory prioritize the development of potentially "winning" ideas that are likely to be evaluated favorably by customers or critics, and that eventually stand to become commercial success stories. Yet, it is difficult to know at the outset how a given idea will turn out. With the advent of crowdsourcing and idea competitions, generating ideas may have become easier, but identifying the most promising ones still remains a real challenge (Rietzschel, Nijstad, & Stroebe, 2006, 2010; Toubia & Florès, 2007).

Firms can attempt to forecast the potential success of an idea by various means (e.g., via customer research and market trend analysis), but these methods can be costly despite their limited effectiveness in predicting the future. After all, only a small fraction of the ideas generated go on to become successful; this is observed across closed and open innovation settings (Chesbrough, 2003), and linear and iterative innovation models (Trott, 2012). Even at P&G, which has often been lauded for its innovation processes, several billion dollars are spent on innovation-related activities each year in the hope of fairly modest organic growth (Brown & Anthony, 2011). The underlying problem, as noted by Barczak, Griffin, and Kahn (2009), is that the current state of innovation research does not make it straightforward for firms to translate theoretical insights into operational processes for identifying promising ideas in practice.

The success of a new idea may depend on a number of different factors, including the characteristics of the innovator (e.g., her expertise and level of political influence), and the market (e.g., current trends and the readiness of customers). Beyond characteristics of the innovator and external influence factors, empirical evidence also suggests that the nature of the raw idea itself – namely its ontological properties such as form and functionality – can be a significant predictor of future success (Cooper, 1988; Cooper, R. Easingwood, C. Edgett, S. Kleinschmidt, E. J. Storey, C., 1994; Goldenberg, Lehmann, & Mazursky, 2001; Kornish & Ulrich, 2014). In light of Barczak et al.'s observation, gaining a better understanding of the extent to which the idea itself may determine success can have significant implications for innovation theory and practice. By focusing on variables derived from the idea itself, significant parsimony may be achieved in predictive models. This in turn could greatly reduce the complexity of innovation processes in a practical setting; innovation managers could potentially identify winning ideas simply from their descriptions. To this end, Goldenberg, Mazursky, and Solomon (1999) have proposed that the essence of what makes an idea successful can be distilled into a handful of abstract "inventive templates" that the idea description may reveal. Kornish and Ulrich (2014) suggest the possibility of assessing ideas based on aggregated "quality scores" given by experts. Meanwhile, studies have shown that analyzing ideas in terms of their feature composition may represent a promising avenue for understanding idea success from a network perspective (Ahn, Ahnert, Bagrow, & Barabási, 2011; Toubia & Netzer, 2017). These represent isolated endeavors in the extant literature, however, while the theoretical foundation and empirical methodology for identifying winning ideas using network analysis remains underdeveloped.

Recognizing this research gap, our paper makes two main contributions. First, we consider how the nature of an idea can contribute to its potential success by providing a new conceptual perspective building on different streams of research. Specifically, we build on the view that the idea itself – or the "idea DNA", as we call it – matters, and can be represented as a network of constituent features. We build on Goldenberg et al.'s work on templates insofar as allowing for the existence of identifiable, well-defined building blocks that can be recombined to form new ideas; this provides an intuitive theoretical point of reference to begin conceptualizing the idea DNA. We further build on insights from research on food-pairing which postulates that certain identifiable network patterns can determine whether a combination of flavors is rated favorably or not (Ahn et al., 2011). We conceptualize the idea DNA as a network of co-occurring idea features, going beyond current approaches that specify institutions, innovators or ideas as nodes of innovation-related networks (Dhar, Geva, Oestreicher-Singer, & Sundararajan, 2014).

Second, based on our conceptual foundation of the idea DNA, we develop a new methodology for identifying winning ideas. Whereas the template method is based on an abstract perspective which is supposed to be independent of an idea's context, we take a more context-aware approach by extracting the idea DNA (an organic set of idea features) from textual idea descriptions. The extraction of idea features can be readily automated and scaled using text mining techniques (Toubia & Netzer, 2017). Empirical evidence from an idea competition dataset suggests that the idea features and related network-based variables (e.g., node centrality) can be strong predictors of idea success. Our findings lead to important theoretical insights and practical implications for firms aiming to build processes for identifying promising ideas.

The remainder of the paper is organized as follows. Section 2 develops the theoretical foundation for the concept of the idea DNA. Section 3 outlines an empirical methodology for operationalizing an idea's DNA as a network of idea features, and deriving network-based predictors of idea success. Section 4 presents the analysis of an idea competition dataset, which serves to validate the network methodology. Finally, Section 5 discusses the implications of our theoretical and empirical contributions, and suggests avenues for future work.

2. Theoretical Foundation

2.1 A Bounded View of Idea Generation

An idea can be understood as an opportunity to create value through investment (Terwiesch & Ulrich, 2009). The identification of promising new ideas plays a central role in the practice of innovation, particularly in the context of new product development (NPD).

Past research suggests that in order to be successful, new ideas must overcome two basic challenges of the innovation problem – namely the abstract and experientially bounded nature of the opportunity space (Beckman & Barry, 2007; Björk & Magnusson, 2009; Koestler, 1989). The opportunity space can intuitively be visualized as a bipartite graph connecting the notional problem space (the full set of problem-related knowledge) to the solution space (the set of all possible solutions). In a typical NPD scenario, the problems and solutions are initially known to the innovator at an abstract level (Jerrard, Trueman, & Newport, 1999). Through an iterative idea generation process of concretization, a problem-solution pair may emerge to become an actionable idea that the firm could implement. Dorst and Cross (2001) formalize the co-evolution of the problem and solution space, while Beckman and Barry (2007) suggest a similar framework of "problem and solution finding and selecting". Crucially, each of the individual features of the final idea arguably captures the aggregation of the various considerations that permeate the idea generation process. The features that constitute the DNA of a winning idea can thus be viewed as the very ingredients of its success.

Goldenberg et al. (1999) suggest that promising new ideas could be generated (and identified) using so-called "inventive templates". While recognizing the ill-defined nature of the opportunity space, the authors especially focus on the benefits of past experience. They argue that inventions across different contexts can be reduced to a set of identifiable and objectively verifiable patterns that may be learned and reused in new situations. This builds on the earlier analysis by Altshuller (1984), which led to the formalization of about 200 identifiable phenomenological links between innovation problems and solutions. Specifically, a template captures the systematic change that transforms an existing product into a new one. The template itself may be constructed from a set of basic operators (exclusion, inclusion, linking, unlinking, splitting and joining). To illustrate the concept, the authors give the example of Domino's Pizza creating a dependency between the two previously unrelated variables of delivery time and price, such that the price of the pizza is reduced if the pizza is delivered late; this so-called "attribute dependency" template is formed by combining the inclusion and linking operators. Empirical findings suggest that ideas based on this template may be considered more innovative by experts (Goldenberg & Mazursky, 1999), and the template-based essence of the idea may also be a significant predictor of success, even when controlling for other factors (Goldenberg et al., 2001).

The template approach can be viewed as part of a broader set of methods, including the use of analogies for innovation (Dahl & Moreau, 2002; Moreau & Dahl, 2005), that involve bounding the solution space. Such methods of bounded creativity have two potential benefits for innovation management. Firstly, these methods provide the means to structure the idea generation process. Whether the ideas are sourced in-house or from an external crowd, those participating in the exercise can use templates to enable the generation of new ideas. Secondly, such methods are, at least in principle, generalizable across different innovation contexts. One could potentially use Goldenberg et al.'s templates to generate new ideas for different types of products.

2.2 From Generic Templates to Context-Aware Idea Features

Despite its merits in facilitating idea generation, the abstract nature of the templates is somewhat problematic when it comes to predicting the success of the generated ideas. How should an innovation manager know which of the ideas are likely to be proclaimed "winners" by an expert jury (as in an idea competition) or the market (upon product launch)? Although templates do not guarantee winners, studies suggest that the use of specific templates is positively correlated with idea success (Goldenberg et al., 2001; Goldenberg et al., 1999). Given a set of generated ideas (some of which may be based on templates), we could attempt to infer the ideas stemming from a set of templates and classify these as promising ideas; this may be one possible way of operationalizing the task of identifying promising ideas in practice. Yet, identifying the presence of templates in a randomly picked idea would typically require the expertise of a trained researcher, which is hard to scale up to the kinds of large idea datasets generated from crowdsourcing initiatives that firms are increasingly beginning to leverage. Automating the detection of templates in a given idea using text mining techniques is also not straightforward due to the abstract semantic properties of each template. The use of templates in practice thus seems to be more suitable for the generation of ideas than the identification of promising ones.

We propose a notable extension of Goldenberg et al.'s work by modifying two aspects of the template-based approach. Our first modification is in shifting the focus from generic templates to what we call "context-aware" features. Goldenberg et al.'s templates could conceivably be meaningful in many contexts (e.g., the attribute dependency template can hold meaning for ideas about cars, cameras, food and so on). By contrast, a feature is context-aware if its semantic meaning derives from a specific context. For example, the technical specifications of a camera are context-aware since they are meaningful in the context of camera design, but may not be generally meaningful in other contexts (e.g., food products). Context-aware features can be concrete/low-level (e.g., technical specifications) or more abstract/high-level (e.g., the taste of a food product). Such context-aware features represent the components of an idea's DNA.

Moreover, our second modification of Goldenberg et al.'s template-based approach is in the automated identification of idea features. We stipulate that, given a context-aware feature and a randomly picked idea, it should be possible to efficiently establish the presence of the feature in the idea. This addresses the issue of scaling the detection of templates/features to large idea databases, and is conceptually closely linked to the mathematical notion of invertible functions.

Specifically, suppose there is a function $G_c(f) = i$ that takes a context c and feature f as input parameters and returns a new contextually relevant idea i as an output; in Goldenberg et al.'s case, f would be a template. Now, crucially, we stipulate that $G_c(f)$ is invertible, i.e., that there exists a function $G_c^{-1}(i) = f$ that can give back the feature f embedded in idea i in context c, and that $G_c^{-1}(i)$ can be computed in an efficient manner. Intuitively, $G_c^{-1}(i)$ in Goldenberg et al.'s work is represented by a human expert that can uncover the presence of a template in an idea via manual analysis, which is difficult to automate and scale. The upshot of successfully implementing our second modification to Goldenberg et al.'s original approach is thus to resolve the problem of scalability in a manner that is practically feasible.

In sum, with the above modifications to the template approach, we extend the research stream characterized by Goldenberg et al.'s work in a number of ways that support the practice of innovation. Firstly, the nature of the templates may cause them to be misinterpreted as a prescriptive and definitive set of ideation tools. There is a danger of practitioners attempting to force-fit existing templates rather than generating newer ones that are more relevant to the innovation problem at hand. The use of context-aware idea features mitigates the risk of such misinterpretation, since the number of features – and hence the opportunity space – is potentially large enough to afford more flexibility in the identification of promising ideas. Secondly, as far as the innovator is concerned, our approach does not impose its own language to the ideation task, but instead reuses the language of the particular innovation context. The staff engaged in NPD at the firm would already be familiar with the language of the context-aware features, which should ease the adoption of our approach in practice. Thirdly, in contrast to the original template approach, our context-aware extension is less at risk of ignoring the rich set of building blocks that the innovators get "for free" from various descriptive data about the product and the associated innovation problem (e.g., lists of components available directly in technical manuals, functional specifications that may be domain-specific, and so on). Fourth, it is difficult to automate the identification of winning ideas using the template approach. With context-aware features, we show that this identification function can be automated in a scalable manner. Taken together, these benefits help address the concern of Barczak et al. (2009) by making the idea DNA concept amenable for practical implementation.

2.3 A Network-Based Configurational View of the Idea DNA

The importance of feature combinations is central to our configurational view of the idea DNA. Rather than looking for the one "killer" feature that may determine an idea's success, we aim for a wider identification process that can capture a set of context-aware features deemed to have survived the iterative evolution of the opportunity space due, in some part, to their interconnections (Dorst & Cross, 2001). The underlying notion that features are related to each other in some way is theoretically appealing. For instance, the network perspective offers an advantage compared to other approaches, such as conjoint analysis, which are constrained by the assumption that features are independent from each other (Green & Srinivasan, 1978; Green & Srinivasan, 2007). The relational view of idea features also readily admits the possibility of innovative ideas emerging from "creative anarchy". Koestler (1989) gives several examples of innovations in human history (e.g., the unification of electricity and magnetism) that arose by combining seemingly unrelated idea features. Note that this act of "connecting the dots" is similar to a template that might be constructed out of linking and unlinking operators (Goldenberg et al., 1999), or the outcome of analogical ideation (Gavetti & Rivkin, 2005), but the nature of the question asked is subtly different. In the case of a template or analogy, one might ask whether transferring a concept from one application to another can create value. With feature combinations, we would instead ask what impact the co-existence of a set of features in the same idea has on its potential for success.

Furthermore, extant literature suggests that the consideration of feature combinations may play an important role in a wide range of innovation problems. In an engineering context, one can imagine trawling through a "scrapyard" (i.e., the opportunity space) to find a compatible set of mechanical parts that form the basis for a novel machine (Altshuller, 1984). Feature combinations may also lead to the development of hybrid products, as in the example of the amphibious car discussed by Goldenberg et al. (1999); in this case, the end result is an innovation that emerges from both destroying and enhancing the road and water-related competencies of the original products (Gatignon, Tushman, Smith, & Anderson, 2002). Meanwhile, if the innovation problem is of a more abstract nature (e.g., deriving an analytical proof), the innovator can actively seek out modular features (e.g., lemmas, auxiliary facts and heuristics) to construct the solution (Pólya, 1971). The freedom of the innovator to combine any components within her reach is a key advantage of recombinant search for innovations (Fleming, 2001; Higgins, 1996). In a similar vein, the practical relevance of conceptualizing the idea DNA as a set of value-creating features is especially evident in the case of software development (Haefliger, Krogh, & Spaeth, 2008). Programmers typically do not write every piece of code from scratch, but instead make use of existing modules of code to craft their software. For example, they may import functions from an open-source library, or use the code made available by an application programming interface. The existence of such highly reusable – yet contextually relevant – blocks of code (i.e., feature combinations) lends credence to our argument that the idea DNA may be an important predictor of success.

The network perspective is ideally suited to the analysis of feature combinations. Networks are conceptualized around the basic notion of relationships between entities (called nodes). The simplest sort of relationship is a dyadic tie that captures a shared characteristic between some pair of nodes in the network (Scott, 2012). Past research has considered innovation-related networks at varying levels of granularity, and the meaning of ties, nodes and the network itself is different at each level. At the highest level, nodes may represent institutions or countries. The Triple Helix model, for example, brings together institutions from the government, industry and academia in a unifying thesis about innovation policies (Etzkowitz & Leydesdorff, 2000). The ties reflect large-scale and often long-term relationships between the institutions, such as alliances for sharing knowledge, material transfer of resources, and collaborations between the public and private sector to facilitate innovation. Note that each of these institutions is made up of the people responsible for actually generating and implementing the innovations. Scholars have consequently studied networks of innovators, and specifically so-called communities of practice (Wenger & Snyder, 2000), in which the nodes have individual agency and the ties may represent anything from shared skills and interests to membership in certain professional groups. One can also construct a network of ideas as nodes, where a tie reflects similarity in some sense. For instance, two ideas or products may share features, be developed by the same firm, co-occur frequently in shopping baskets, and so on. Note that, in contrast to networks of people, nodes in an idea network do not have agency and the ties between ideas reflect the aggregate preferences of agents existing outside the network (Dhar et al., 2014; Leung, Agarwal, Konana, & Kumar, 2016).

Going a level deeper, we propose a network of idea features, in which the components that make up the idea are themselves exposed as nodes. Ties in a feature network reflect the aggregate preferences of external agents (e.g., an expert panel or customers) about the idea features and combinations thereof. Importantly, each feature in the network is represented by a single node even if it appears in multiple ideas. This allows for the idea DNA to be shared across several potentially diverse ideas, which is in line with our motivation to "crack the code" of successful ideas by making their interconnected features observable. While Haefliger et al. (2008) did not use network analysis in their study of code reuse in software development, their findings suggest that there is conceptual merit in going to this level of detail. In social networking literature, researchers studying cross-cultural culinary patterns have shown that constructing a network of food ingredients can reveal combinations of ingredients that are particularly salient for the success of a recipe (Ahn et al., 2011; Teng, Lin, & Adamic, 2012). Meanwhile, Toubia and Netzer (2017) have shown the value of using ingredient-level semantic networks to analyze the success of ideas in an innovation context. In particular, they build a network of co-occurring word stems and derive a measure for the prototypicality of an idea based on the edge weight distribution of the corresponding subnetwork of word stems. They find empirical evidence for the so-called "beauty in averageness" effect, such that successful ideas tend to balance novelty and familiarity. However, there is generally a paucity of empirical studies of feature networks in innovation literature.

By transferring the implications of the network perspective to the context of innovation and NPD, we thus argue that the network perspective at the feature level is worth exploring for at least three reasons. Firstly, we extend current theory by exposing idea features that may be shared across ideas, and provide an intuitive exposition for this approach using networks. Secondly, the idea DNA concept can extend the findings of Goldenberg et al.'s work on templates and create a practical foundation for the operationalization of idea selection processes within firms. Given that winning ideas are hard to come by but have a potentially significant upside, we argue that the stakes are high enough from a managerial perspective to pay more attention to feature combinations. Finally, we are at an ideal point in time to tackle innovation from the perspective of features. Over the years, scholars and practitioners have gained a better understanding of the role of building blocks and combinations thereof (e.g., templates and reusable software code) in the development of promising ideas. Meanwhile, technological advances have created new ways of deriving idea features (e.g., text mining, machine learning techniques, semantic networks). Today's technology also allows us to practically deal with the potentially high dimensionality of the feature set. For instance, algorithms have been optimized to do the feature selection task in a way that is practically attractive (i.e., cheap, fast and accurate). We are therefore well-placed to extend the current state of innovation research by exploiting new technical possibilities.

3. Network-Based Methodology

3.1 Representing the Idea DNA as a Network

To facilitate an exposition of the DNA of successful ideas from a network perspective, we outline a methodology to represent ideas as a network of nodes and edges in a graph-theoretical sense.

Our empirical study described in Section 4 relates to an idea competition hosted by a global consumer goods company to source new ideas for chocolate bars. Thus, to aid the concrete understanding of the concepts and its validation in the study, we use the same idea competition as an example here. A sample idea submitted in the competition is shown in Appendix A1. Ideas for chocolate bars may involve the innovative use of food ingredients (e.g., flavors of chocolate), decorative packaging, or messaging via logos and motifs. In this context, we can view an idea's DNA as being composed of several features such as size, visual appeal, packaging, functional innovativeness and more. Note that such conceptual features can be generated using automated topic-modeling methods such as Latent Dirichlet Allocation (Blei, Ng, & Jordan, 2003), as we do in this paper; this can significantly increase the scalability of feature generation in particular, and allow us to highly automate our entire methodology in general, for large datasets.

Moreover, the features can be coded dichotomously (e.g., whether an idea contains an ingredient or not), or using a scale to capture the feature's intensity (e.g., level of visual appeal). With the aim of facilitating ease of implementation by practitioners in mind, we follow Toubia and Florès (2007) and only work with dichotomized variables in this paper, although treatment of other types of variables would be similar. Also, it is arguably not unreasonable to expect the use of dichotomized variables in a managerial setting. For example, dichotomization may speed up the coding process, and a binary outcome variable (e.g., an idea is rated either "good" or "bad") may simplify the process of idea selection. Table 1 shows an imaginary sample dataset of some ideas (1 = feature present, 0 = feature not present). Note that, while some features are inherently binary (e.g., "has dark chocolate"), we can assume that the other variables have been dichotomized during the coding procedure. We will use the dataset in Table 1 for illustrating our methodology in this section.

Idea ID	Features					Success Variable
	Has Dark Chocolate	Has Fruit Flavor	Visually Appealing	Decorative Packaging	Functionally Innovative	Expert Rating
A	1	0	1	0	1	1
B	1	1	0	0	0	0
C	0	1	1	1	0	1
D	0	1	0	0	0	0
E	1	0	1	0	0	0

Table 1: Sample Idea Dataset

We can conceptualize the idea DNA as a network of features that co-occur across the different ideas. An edge between two nodes indicates that the features co-occur in an idea. For instance, in idea A, the following features co-occur: dark chocolate, visual appeal and functional innovativeness. Meanwhile, in idea E, dark chocolate and visual appeal also co-occur. By considering the entire idea dataset in this manner and merging the resulting sub-networks, the full network of co-occurring features can be derived.

3.2 Generating Network-Based Predictors of Idea Success

Based on the feature network, we can operationalize the analysis of the DNA of successful ideas at the feature-level, by considering which individual features are the most important for idea success. We can represent the mapping of features to ideas in Table 1 as a matrix,

$$X = \begin{pmatrix} 1 & 0 & 1 & 0 & 1 \\ 1 & 1 & 0 & 0 & 0 \\ 0 & 1 & 1 & 1 & 0 \\ 0 & 1 & 0 & 0 & 0 \\ 1 & 0 & 1 & 0 & 0 \end{pmatrix},$$

where $X_{i,j}$ denotes the presence of feature j in idea i in matrix X. Operationally, we now wish to generate a $n \times n$ co-occurrence matrix M, where n is the number of unique features in the dataset. Each element $M_{i,j}$ could represent the co-occurrence frequency of features i and j across all ideas in the dataset. For example, in our case, $M_{1,3} = 2$, denoting the number of ideas that have dark chocolate and are visually appealing. From X we thus derive such a matrix,

$$M = \begin{pmatrix} 0 & 1 & 2 & 0 & 1 \\ 0 & 0 & 1 & 1 & 0 \\ 0 & 0 & 0 & 1 & 1 \\ 0 & 0 & 0 & 0 & 0 \\ 0 & 0 & 0 & 0 & 0 \end{pmatrix}.$$

Subsequently, M can be conceptualized as an undirected weighted graph (with 5 nodes and 7 edges in our case), from which several network-based measures can be derived at the feature level (Scott, 2012). Some network measures, such as degree centrality and betweenness, can help us identify highly central features that co-occur with many other features, or those that act as structures holes to bridge the gap between feature clusters. In our matrix M, for instance, the weighted degree of the first feature ("Has Dark Chocolate"), third feature ("Visually Appealing") and fifth feature ("Functionally Innovative") are 4, 5 and 2, respectively. Other measures, such as modularity, can help us better understand the community structure within the feature network. The modularity class of a node reflects the cluster of the network a node is likely to belong to, beyond what would be expected in a random graph (Blondel, Guillaume, Lambiotte, & Lefebvre, 2008); the number of unique modularity classes represented by an idea's feature set thus provides an indication of the idea's feature breadth. Formal definitions of the network measures used in this paper are shown in Appendix A8.

Operationally, we aggregate the feature-level network measures at the idea-level to be able to include them in the classification model (in which each observation represents a unique idea); we henceforth refer to these aggregate measures as *feature network indices* (FNIs). One approach to deriving FNIs is to take the average of the feature-level network measures for each idea, effectively using a popular measure of central tendency as a heuristic for aggregation. For example, from the first row in X we see that the DNA of idea A consists of three features: dark chocolate, visual appeal, and functional innovativeness. Now we can take an aggregated network measure (e.g., average degree of an idea's features) and include it as an additional predictor variable in the classification model. The average weighted degree of feature for idea A would thus be $(4 + 5 + 2)/3 = 3.67$. Similarly, other FNIs can be constructed by summarizing feature-level network measures per idea. Henceforth, we shall refer to the coded features (such as those shown in Table 1) as "base features" to distinguish them from the FNIs.

3.3 Using Random Forests to Classify Successful Ideas

Having generated the base features and FNIs, we can build models to predict the success of each idea. From a managerial perspective, we may want to know which ideas are likely to receive better ratings in an idea competition or achieve higher sales upon market launch. To analyze the usefulness of including FNIs in the models, we can compare reduced models (i.e., using only base features or FNIs) to full models (using all features).

In this paper, we use random forests (RFs) based on decision trees to model the success variable (e.g., expert ratings) using the base features and FNIs as predictors. Breiman (2001) gives a formal overview of RFs and the intuition is as follows. Rather than building just one tree to model the outcome variable, k such trees (typically hundreds or thousands) are built by bootstrapping samples (with replacement) from a training dataset T. The basic motivation behind this approach is that, while each of these k trees may over/under-fit the data to some extent, aggregating the predictions of the k individual trees should give a more accurate prediction result for the overall forest (Breiman, 1996). Operationally, such bootstrap aggregation (or "bagging") could mean taking an average of all k predictions, or using some form of voting among the trees to calibrate the features in the final predictive algorithm of the forest.

Note that each bootstrap sample leaves about 37% of the observations unused. The size of this out-of-bag sample can be confirmed mathematically, since the probability of not picking the same observation in any of N draws is $(1 - 1/N)^N$, which converges to $1/e \approx 0.37$ as N approaches infinity. Crucially, the random forest procedure thus elegantly provides us with data for holdout testing in the form of the out-of-bag sample. In general, the testing data can be obtained by independently sampling from the same underlying distribution as that of the training set (Breiman, 1996). The out-of-bag sample appears to satisfy this requirement and the out-of-bag error (θ) can be shown to be an unbiased estimate of the generalization error for the RF. Then $1 - \theta$ gives us a measure of an RF's overall predictive accuracy (Hastie, Tibshirani, & Friedman J., 2009), i.e., the number of correct predictions (true positives and true negatives) out of all predictions.

The use of tree-based RFs is common in the domain of machine learning, and has a number of advantages over traditional econometric approaches to classification such as logistic regressions. Decision trees are well-suited for modelling nonlinearities and interactions, and can effectively handle missing data (Varian, 2014). Trees also outperform logistic regressions on high-dimensional data (Perlich, Provost, & Simonoff, 2003). After all, the RF approach seeks to improve the predictive accuracy generating an ensemble of several models and combining their predictions. Our choice of RFs also fits neatly into our overarching story of idea configurations and networks; a forest of decision trees is essentially a manifestation of a certain kind of network topology.

Furthermore, to identify the most important features for classifying the ideas, we can make use of the Gini indices that emerges naturally from the RF algorithm (Archer & Kimes, 2008). We use the implementation of RFs provided by Liaw and Wiener (2002), in which $\sqrt{p}$ features are randomly sampled as candidates at every split while forming each separate decision tree. Splitting on important features is associated with a reduction in node impurity. The Gini index is a measure of the total decrease in node impurities due to splitting on a given variable, averaged across all k trees in the RF. Thus, the higher the Gini index for a predictor variable, the more salient it is for classifying the outcome variable.

4. Empirical Evidence

4.1 Data

We partnered with a European innovation consultancy that facilitates the execution of large idea competitions for firms across a range of industry sectors via a bespoke online platform. Table 2 summarizes the key information for an idea competition dataset we obtained, which was previously also qualitatively analyzed by Jawecki, Gebauer, and Mathis-Alig (2013). Ideas were evaluated based on the ratings of an expert jury panel (3 subject matter experts and firm executives). The chocolate idea competition also allowed the participant community to rate ideas. In all cases, ratings were given on a Likert scale of 0-5 (worst to best), and expected to reflect the overall performance of the idea across typical criteria (e.g., novelty, relevance, feasibility).

	Dataset: Chocolate Ideas
Competition Aim	An international manufacturer of foods and beverages wants to reinvent the design of chocolate bars to enhance customer experience. Ideas for new designs can explore the full breadth of opportunities for innovation (e.g., food ingredients, form, branding, packaging).
Participants	Participation was open to all, with a cash prize incentive; 1,078 individuals from 69 different countries signed up to take part.
Timeline	Competition launched on 6 November 2012 and the ideas were collected over a period of 6 weeks. Overall 4,488 hours were spent by participants and experts on submitting, discussing, and evaluating the ideas on the platform.
Number of Rated Ideas	468
Idea Evaluation	Expert ratings and community ratings

Table 2: Overview of Idea Competition Dataset

Table 3 presents the descriptive statistics of the ideas. To get a sense of the overall idea success in the chocolate competition, we construct a combined rating by taking a 50-50 weighted average of the expert and community ratings. Both ratings seem to follow a roughly normal distribution and are positively correlated with each other, although the community appears to be slightly more lenient than the experts.

The binary outcome variables to represent idea success are derived by dichotomizing the ratings around their respective sample means.

Rating	N	Mean	SD	Min	Max
		Raw			
Expert	468	2.614	0.603	1.000	4.714
Community	468	3.466	0.654	1.000	5.000
Combined	468	3.040	0.518	1.000	4.382
		Dichotomized			
Expert	468	0.491	0.500	0.000	1.000
Community	468	0.532	0.500	0.000	1.000
Combined	468	0.519	0.500	0.000	1.000

Table 3: Descriptive Statistics of Idea Ratings

4.2 Derivation of Idea Features

In order to apply the network-based methodology described in Section 3, the ideas have to be coded to derive idea-level features. Specifically, we make use of Latent Dirichlet Allocation (LDA), as described by Blei et al. (2003), to extract features (or topics) from the entire idea description text corpus of the idea competition. Unlike deterministic rule-based text-mining techniques, LDA represents an unsupervised stochastic method of pattern detection. LDA assumes that the full text corpus has been generated via a probabilistic process that chooses words from a set of latent topics. The probability distribution of each topic determines the words that are chosen. Our objective of extracting features from the text corpus thus amounts to the discovery of topics.

We implement LDA as follows. To begin with, all n idea description texts $D_{1..n}$ from the competition are concatenated into a single string of text (i.e., the corpus). This text is then cleaned by removing all stop-words (e.g., "a", "an", "by", etc.) and punctuation symbols, and lemmatization is used to reduce the raw set of words to their base forms (i.e., lemmas). For example, the lemma of the inflected words "loving" and "loved" is "love". These lemmas can then be stored as a uniquely indexed dictionary of m terms $W_{1..m}$. Removing stop-words and deriving lemmas are typical preprocessing steps in natural language processing. Formally, the entire text corpus can now be represented as a matrix C of n rows (one for each idea text) and m columns (one for each lemma). The element C_{ij} stores the frequency count of word W_j in idea text D_i. We can then iteratively run the LDA algorithm to generate k features (topics) for the entire text corpus. Operationally, each feature is

64

represented by a set of related words, such that any given word W_j can be mapped to some feature F_k. We can constrain the algorithm by specifying upper bounds on the number of features and the number of words per feature that we wish to discover. Bounding the number of features and words per feature yields a particular LDA specification, and means that only the topics that are probabilistically the best fit for the text corpus (and words that are the best fit for a given topic) beyond a certain threshold of fitness will be derived.

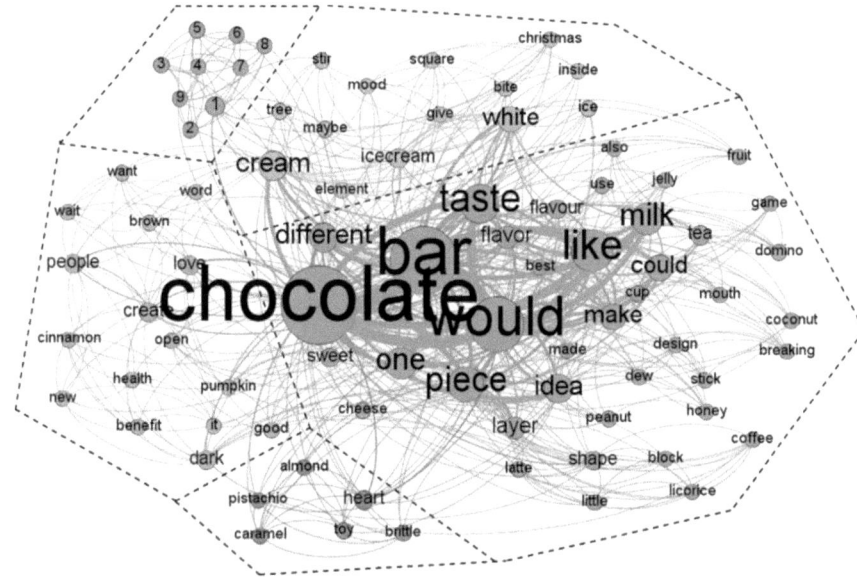

Figure 1: Word Network for 20 Topic/10 Words LDA Specification

Topic	Word 1	Word 2	Word 3	Word 4	Word 5	Word 6	Word 7	Word 8	Word 9	Word 10
"Summer"	chocolate	bar	different	ice	cream	would	white	heart	flavor	element
"Love"	chocolate	bar	good	idea	love	open	sweet	one	pumpkin	layer
"Social"	chocolate	word	want	wait	create	love	people	bar	cream	brown
"Honey"	chocolate	bar	would	piece	peanut	idea	taste	make	honey	made
"Creation"	chocolate	would	bar	stick	idea	design	one	like	dew	breaking
"Unique"	chocolate	bar	would	idea	taste	use	milk	jelly	one	different
"Nutty"	chocolate	pistachio	would	almond	piece	caramel	idea	heart	toy	brittle
"Quantifiable"	2	chocolate	4	3	5	1	8	6	7	9

65

"Pieces"	chocolate	bar	milk	white	would	like	different	one	flavor	piece
"Nature"	christmas	chocolate	1	icecream	tree	cream	stir	maybe	white	bar
"Fruity"	chocolate	bar	like	milk	fruit	icecream	taste	white	would	flavour
"Tasty"	chocolate	like	taste	make	bar	best	flavor	would	piece	could
"Sweet"	chocolate	milk	would	bar	cream	taste	sweet	shape	like	cheese
"Dark"	chocolate	block	piece	licorice	coffee	shape	latte	layer	dark	little
"Shape"	cream	chocolate	bar	taste	inside	give	square	bite	different	mood
"Health"	chocolate	new	bar	cinnamon	create	it	people	dark	benefit	health
"Layering"	chocolate	would	bar	one	like	taste	layer	piece	make	flavour
"Novelty"	chocolate	bar	would	piece	tea	cup	coconut	could	mouth	like
"Different"	chocolate	bar	would	different	like	could	milk	taste	make	one
"Game"	chocolate	bar	like	would	milk	also	could	tea	domino	game

Table 4: Feature Generation for 20 Topic/10 Words LDA Specification

Table 4 shows the results of running the LDA algorithm specifying the generation of 20 topics (features) consisting of 10 words each. Figure 1 depicts the network of words that co-occur in a topic, to illustrate inter-word relationships underlying the LDA analysis. Node size reflects the weighted degree measure, the thickness of edges corresponds to the co-occurrence frequencies of the respective features, and the dashed lines mark the boundaries between network communities (modularity classes). We shall use this 20 topics/10 words specification as the main example to walk through our findings in the following section, and summarize the results of other LDA specifications as robustness checks in the Appendix. Note that we have relaxed the sensitivity of the LDA algorithm to allow regional variations in English spelling (e.g., "flavor" and "flavour") or minor grammatical issues (e.g., "icecream"). Also, the algorithm itself merely labels the discovered topics as "Topic 1", "Topic 2" and so on. To give the topics (word lists) some semantic meaning, we provide indicative qualitative labels for the topics in Table 4 based on an exploratory analysis of the occurrence of the topics and their constituent words in the idea dataset. It is worth emphasizing, however, that the actual labels themselves do not affect the mechanics of our automated methodology.

Since we conceptually hold that the DNA of success can exist to varying degrees in all ideas within a shared context (e.g., the design of chocolate bars), the LDA-based features are derived at the level of the entire text corpus that consists of all idea descriptions in our dataset. We then take the approach of testing for set membership to map these features to individual ideas. As each idea D_i is essentially a set of its constituent words, if $D_i \cap F_k \neq \emptyset$, then feature k is present in idea i. For example, the feature "health" is present in an idea if its constituent words are present in the idea description. Furthermore, our LDA-based operationalization of features has two important implications. First, the word lists of two different features may have some words in common (e.g., "chocolate" and "bar" in the case of our data, as seen in Table 4). Such common words cannot uniquely identify features in an idea description. Second, a feature may be more prevalent in one idea than another. In our text-mining context, feature prevalence can be defined as a function of the breadth and frequency of occurrence of a feature's constituent words in a given idea description. To address the above implications, we define the prevalence of feature F_k in idea D_i as the mean of the word occurrence frequencies of each word in F_k that appears in D_i. We then standardize the feature prevalence, and dichotomize it around the sample mean of the respective feature to derive the final set of base features. Thus, the identification of a feature in an idea description will be driven by the presence of words that are unique to the said feature.

The methodology is implemented using a combination of standard programming languages (R and python) and the software tool Gephi for conducting the network analysis (Bastian, Heymann, Jacomy, & others, 2009). Specifically, we construct FNIs based on two node-level network measures – weighted degree centrality and modularity (see Appendix A8 for formal definitions of these network measures). Intuitively, the average weighted degree of an idea's features gives an indication of how central these features are with respect to the full set of features in the idea dataset. The number of unique modularity classes of an idea highlights the diversity of the features that make up the idea. Table 5 reports the descriptive statistics for the base features and feature network indices (FNIs) that are obtained by applying the methodology described in Section 3. Note that while each dichotomized feature occurs in about 40-50% of the ideas in our dataset, the actual distribution and combinations of features vary across ideas. We show descriptive results for features derived from other LDA specifications as robustness checks in Appendix A2-A3. Moreover, Table 6 shows the number of times a pair of base features co-occurs within an idea description. We find that this co-occurrence frequency in our dataset tends to be 50-160 and is about 93 on average.

VARIABLES	Frequency of Occurrences across Ideas	
Base Features (= LDA Topic)	**Absolute**	**Relative**
Summer	203	43.4%

Love	219	46.8%
Social	211	45.1%
Honey	209	44.7%
Creation	198	42.3%
Unique	207	44.2%
Nutty	235	50.2%
Quantifiable	240	51.3%
Pieces	203	43.4%
Nature	236	50.4%
Fruity	207	44.2%
Tasty	205	43.8%
Sweet	198	42.3%
Dark	232	49.6%
Shape	219	46.8%
Health	221	47.2%
Layering	201	42.9%
Novelty	193	41.2%
Different	211	45.1%
Tasty	198	42.3%
Feature Network Indices (FNIs)	**Mean**	**SD**
Average Weighted Degree	819.341	177.378
Unique Modularity Classes	1.927	0.26
N = 468 ideas		

Table 5: Descriptive Statistics for 20 Topic/10 Words LDA Specification

	Summer	Love	Social	Honey	Creation	Unique	Nutty	Quant.	Pieces	Nature
Summer	0	90	87	85	86	104	103	94	115	120
Love	0	0	128	96	102	107	101	119	82	140
Social	0	0	0	72	80	76	94	124	55	155
Honey	0	0	0	0	105	112	124	73	89	78
Creation	0	0	0	0	0	111	105	64	100	79
Unique	0	0	0	0	0	0	104	75	119	77

Nutty	0	0	0	0	0	0	0	140	101	93
Quant.	0	0	0	0	0	0	0	0	75	149
Pieces	0	0	0	0	0	0	0	0	0	82
Nature	0	0	0	0	0	0	0	0	0	0
Fruity	0	0	0	0	0	0	0	0	0	0
Tasty	0	0	0	0	0	0	0	0	0	0
Sweet	0	0	0	0	0	0	0	0	0	0
Dark	0	0	0	0	0	0	0	0	0	0
Shape	0	0	0	0	0	0	0	0	0	0
Health	0	0	0	0	0	0	0	0	0	0
Layering	0	0	0	0	0	0	0	0	0	0
Novelty	0	0	0	0	0	0	0	0	0	0
Different	0	0	0	0	0	0	0	0	0	0
Game	0	0	0	0	0	0	0	0	0	0

	Fruity	Tasty	Sweet	Dark	Shape	Health	Layering	Novelty	Different	Game
Summer	101	89	94	78	106	97	66	74	90	82
Love	57	66	64	105	127	129	86	57	72	52
Social	70	55	68	104	128	150	55	58	57	67
Honey	90	124	92	84	98	86	124	98	94	71
Creation	91	99	93	54	80	84	106	110	101	109
Unique	112	95	106	69	109	83	105	71	136	90
Nutty	86	98	85	143	83	96	92	107	77	90
Quant.	94	67	81	158	111	120	65	63	80	84
Pieces	115	114	99	92	72	70	109	94	126	105
Nature	87	60	76	127	139	154	59	67	73	81
Fruity	0	113	144	78	82	67	109	94	130	122
Tasty	0	0	107	83	78	66	148	133	142	109
Sweet	0	0	0	79	80	64	104	88	115	116
Dark	0	0	0	0	101	108	91	95	77	74
Shape	0	0	0	0	0	129	87	64	97	61
Health	0	0	0	0	0	0	66	63	68	78
Layering	0	0	0	0	0	0	0	112	131	86

Novelty	0	0	0	0	0	0	0	0	106	133
Different	0	0	0	0	0	0	0	0	0	124
Game	0	0	0	0	0	0	0	0	0	0

Table 6: Feature Co-occurrence in Ideas for 20 Topic/10 Words LDA Specification

4.3 Results

Having generated the base features and FNIs, we are now in a position to build models to predict the success of each idea. As described in Section 3.2, we use tree-based random forests (RFs) to build the predictive models. Table 7 shows the predictive results for the outcome variable "Expert Ratings" across different sets of predictor variables (base, FNIs, and combined); in each case, the predictive model is trained on a forest of 500 decision trees. Recall that predictive accuracy is equivalent to $1 - \theta$, where θ denotes the out-of-bag error rate (Hastie et al., 2009). We find that, using base features only or base + FNIs as the predictive set, the true positive rate, true negative rate and overall accuracy are similar (around 52%). Using a predictive set of FNIs only, however, yields a higher true positive rate (58.26%) and a lower true negative rate (44.54%), and gives an overall accuracy similar to that of the other predictive sets. These results suggest that FNIs are more "optimistic" predictors than base features. The FNI measure is less likely to be susceptible to false negatives (i.e., not correctly identifying a successful idea), but will be more vulnerable to false positives by giving an unsuccessful idea the benefit of the doubt.

We report a summary of overall predictive accuracies for several specifications of outcome and predictor variables as robustness checks in Appendix A4. Note that the expected accuracy differs by the type of outcome variable denoting success. For example, about 49.1% of the ideas in the chocolate dataset are classified as "successful" by the dichotomized expert rating variable, so we would expect a random guess to correctly predict the success outcome of an idea 49.1% of the time. Interestingly, Table 7 suggests that the combined features (base + FNIs) of the 20 topic/10 word LDA specification yield a 7-8% higher predictive accuracy than the random expectation. In fact, according to Table A4 in the Appendix, the actual predictive accuracies exceed the random expectation across several combinations of LDA parameters and predictor types significantly ($p < 0.01$), which is remarkable considering that we only use predictors derived from the idea itself (Kornish & Ulrich, 2014). The results suggest that the choice of LDA parameters and predictors affects the predictive performance. Also, based on Table A4, using more information-rich LDA parameters (i.e., more topics and more words per topic)

70

appears to improve predictive accuracy. Similarly, models that use both the base features and FNIs tend to outperform simpler models, especially for the richer LDA parameter choices. These results are well-aligned with our theoretical expectation that more information can lead to better predictive accuracy.

Accuracy of Predicting Outcome Variable: Expert Rating	Predictors		
	Base only	FNIs only	Base + FNIs
True Positive Rate (TPR = accuracy of predicting *successful* idea correctly)	52.6%	58.3%	51.7%
True Negative Rate (TNR = accuracy of predicting *unsuccessful* idea correctly)	52.1%	44.5%	53.8%
Overall Accuracy (accuracy of predicting idea success correctly)	52.4%	51.3%	52.8%
TPR and TNR are also known as sensitivity and specificity, respectively. *Results are based on the roughly 37% out-of-bag sample of N = 468 ideas (i.e., about 172 unused observations per bootstrap sample). We use forests consisting of 500 trees.*			

Table 7: Summary of Predictive Results for 20 Topic/10 Words LDA specification

Furthermore, we can use Gini indices to identify the best predictors of idea success. As explained by Archer and Kimes (2008), the more important the predictor, the greater its Gini index will be. Besides the absolute Gini index, the difference between the Gini indices of predictors that are next to each other in a Gini-based ranking also represents a useful measure of variable importance (we call this the "jump in variable importance"). Figure 2 graphically maps out the variable importance of the predictors derived from the 20 topic/10 word LDA specification in the case of predicting expert ratings. Certain base features (e.g., "Shape" and "Summer") and the FNI "Average Weighted Degree" stand out in Figure 2 as especially important predictors of idea success. Appendix A5 provides a table of the exact Gini values, which shows that the rankings appear to be fairly stable across predictor sets, although the importance of the FNI "Average Weighted Degree" increases considerably in the predictor set containing both base features and FNIs. In econometrics, one might also typically look at beta coefficients to gauge the notional importance of predictor variables in a classification model. As such, we compare the Gini-based rankings to analogous Probit models (see Appendix A6), and find that predictors with high Gini-based rankings can be statistically significant in the Probit models as well.

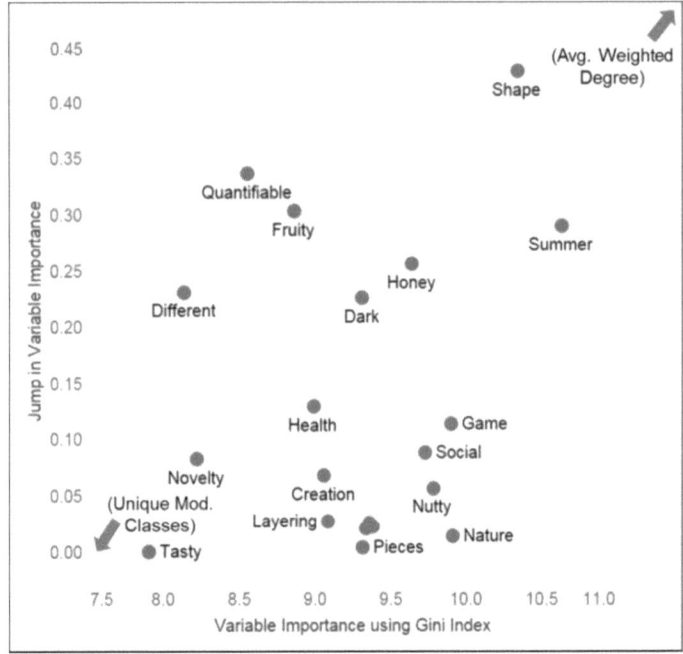

Figure 2: Predictor Variable Importance for 20 Topic/10 Words LDA Specification

Overall, the analysis of Gini-based rankings for several combinations of outcomes and predictors shown in Table A4 yields three main findings. Firstly, only about 20% of the features in each case appear to largely drive the idea success. These features tend to represent concepts like shape, seasonality and social interaction. Secondly, the centrality-related FNI (average weighted degree of features in an idea) is consistently among the top 2 best predictors, when all base and FNI predictors are included in the model; this is well-aligned with our underlying argument in Sections 2-3 of adopting a network perspective to understand the makeup of successful ideas. Thirdly, the diversity-related FNI – the number of unique modularity classes represented by the set of base features in an idea – becomes a more salient predictor of success as the LDA parameters become more information-rich (more topics and more words). This is intuitively to be

72

expected, since a richer feature set is likely to show greater semantic diversity, which in turn is leveraged by the modularity-based FNI.

Finally, recall that Toubia and Netzer (2017) find evidence of the "beauty in averageness" effect in the evaluation of ideas, suggesting that ideas which balance familiarity and uniqueness tend to be rated more favorably. We complement this work by analyzing the extent to which the uniqueness of an idea's base feature correlates with its ability to predict idea success. One way to derive a metric for the uniqueness of base features in our setting is to use the fact that the word lists of topics generated by LDA may overlap. For example, words such as "chocolate", "bar" and "taste" are shared by several topics. We can produce a set W_T of the top N most common words across topics, and define the uniqueness $U(F_i)$ of a topic (base feature) F_i as the number of words F_i that *do not occur* in W_T. Features with a high $U(F_i)$ can thus be considered unique in the sense that they consist of few commonly occurring words. Figure A7 in the Appendix shows the 25 most common words for the 20 topic/10 word LDA specification, and Table A7 maps the uniqueness of topics to their predictive importance. Interestingly, we find that the more unique topics tend to be better predictors of idea success, and this finding appears to be robust to the cutoff N for defining the set of most common words.

5. Conclusion and Discussion

5.1 Summary of Contributions

The identification of potentially successful ideas is a key challenge for scholars and practitioners of innovation, especially in the context of new product development. Extant literature suggests that the ingredients of the idea itself may yield important variables for explaining the success of the idea (Kornish & Ulrich, 2014). However, there has been a relative paucity of innovation and marketing literature investigating the nature of the idea further – our paper aims to address this gap by taking a network perspective. In doing so, we broadly make two main contributions that are complementary to one another.

Our first contribution is to develop a configurational theory about the idea itself, which suggests that an idea's compositional features may be strong predictors of success. We especially draw on the work of Goldenberg et al. (1999) that outlines the use of templates to generate innovative ideas. Fundamentally, Goldenberg et al. propose that a new idea can be constructed from one or more high-level building blocks (templates). Retaining this basic intuition, we conceptualize an idea as a complex network of context-aware features. These features may be granular and concrete (e.g., technical specifications of a product), or coarse and abstract (e.g., sensory appeal, emotional associations). Unlike other external variables related to the idea, such as the innovator or market conditions, we hold that the idea's network of features (i.e., its DNA) is ontologically inseparable from the idea itself. Within this context, we argue that identifying successful ideas in new product development is tantamount to identifying ideas with a "winning" DNA. Successful ideas need not be particularly extraordinary, and may avoid the risk of being perceived as "too far out" (Mueller, Melwani, & Goncalo, 2012; Toubia & Netzer, 2017). Analyzing idea features fosters a better understanding of why some ideas are more successful than others. Considering the full set of ideas within a specific context or idea competition also lets us take advantage of the content of ideas that do not belong to the group of winning ideas. In fact, even unsuccessful ideas might contain some winning features, implying the value of feature combinations which network analysis can help us to capture.

Our second contribution is thus to develop a network-based methodology for operationalizing the identification of winning ideas. The network perspective emerges naturally out of the configurational view of ideas, and is ideally suited to the analysis of – oftentimes complex – feature combinations. Previous innovation research has used networks to represent relationships between institutions, innovators and ideas (Dhar et al., 2014; Etzkowitz & Leydesdorff, 2000; Wenger & Snyder, 2000). Building on some isolated endeavors in extant research (Ahn et al., 2011; Toubia & Netzer, 2017), we go one level deeper by proposing a network of the individual idea features themselves. Features are represented as nodes, and two features share an edge if they co-occur in some idea; the edge weights reflect the number of co-occurrences for each pair of nodes. We allow several ideas to be represented in the same feature network, which is intuitively appealing since it captures the notion of different ideas sharing portions of one another's DNA. We can use the feature network to produce idea-level network statistics (FNIs), and use all of these explanatory variables to build predictive models for idea success. Although any number of different models from traditional econometrics or machine learning can be used to classify successful ideas (Varian, 2014), we focus on tree-based random forests (RFs). The configurational nature of RFs fits elegantly into our broader narrative of idea features and networks in this paper.

We validate the idea DNA theory and network-based methodology using an idea competition dataset about new ideas related to chocolate bars. The dataset consists of textual idea descriptions along with their ratings (i.e., the success variables). To demonstrate the possibility of automating our methodology, we use LDA-based topic modeling to derive the base features of ideas. Using text mining, we construct a co-occurrence network of these base features across the idea competition dataset, and derive network-based measures (FNIs) related to the centrality and breadth of the base features of each idea. We then build tree-based RF models to predict the impact of the base features and FNIs on idea success. This empirical investigation leads to two overarching findings. First, the evidence suggests that an idea's base features (i.e., its ingredients) can be salient predictors of success. Second, the FNIs (i.e., the aggregate, network-based measures derived from the base features across the idea dataset) also appear to be strong predictors of idea success. These findings are well-aligned with our theoretical argument of the idea DNA, which emphasizes the relevance of an idea's complex, configurational makeup (as represented by its features) to its potential for success. The RF predictive models are especially well-suited to capturing the nonlinearities and diverse interaction effects across several features (Varian, 2014).

5.2 Theoretical and Managerial Implications

Our empirical results suggest that a network perspective of the idea DNA can lead to a more nuanced and fruitful understanding of the key ingredients driving idea success. Our work provides structure to the intuitive appeal of connectedness between and within ideas, thus augmenting and uniting a number of perspectives from extant theory. For example, theories of recombinant search (Fleming, 2001; Higgins, 1996) have previously been extended through the use of analogies and templates to facilitate creative problem-solving (Gavetti & Rivkin, 2005; Goldenberg & Mazursky, 1999; Goldenberg et al., 1999). Yet, while the theoretical value of recombination in approaching the problem of idea selection has become increasingly apparent, the combinations themselves have typically been analyzed at a high level. For example, Goldenberg et al. (1999) derive abstract templates, while Dyer, Gregersen, and Christensen (2009) identify broad features of an innovator that may translate to the success of an idea. Our configurational notion of the idea DNA and the validation of the related empirical methodology imply that network-based thinking can help uncover new predictors of idea success at a deeper level. Our work implies that there is theoretical merit in emphasizing a relational view at the level of context-aware idea features. Thus, in synthesizing the extant research, our theoretical conceptualization of the idea DNA takes us a step closer to piecing together the puzzle of successful ideas in new product development.

Moreover, our network-based methodology implies that the same feature may occur in multiple ideas, namely that different ideas can share the same DNA. This is not only intuitively appealing but also contributes to our theoretical understanding of "similarity" between ideas. For instance, sharing features or belonging to the same latent cluster (in the sense of topic modeling) indicate similarity between different ideas, the magnitude of which may vary based on the amount of overlap. Extant theories suggest that the real opportunity space in ideation (i.e., the set of unique ideas) may be smaller than it first appears due to several redundancies across ideas (Kornish & Ulrich, 2011; Sommer & Loch, 2004). Such redundancies could be viewed negatively in the case of idea generation, where idea diversity may be an important goal. When idea selection is the goal, however, such redundancies may be desirable, since they reveal latent connections between disparate ideas, and thus represent a useful criterion for identification. Crucially, the success of one idea could imply the potential for success of other similar ideas. This theoretical implication becomes quite significant when we consider the complexity of open innovation and co-creation (Chesbrough, 2003; Prahalad & Ramaswamy, 2004b; Prahalad & Ramaswamy, 2004a). With several innovators developing ideas simultaneously, it becomes increasingly important to cut through the noise and accurately classify the winning ideas in the opportunity space.

Finally, from a managerial perspective, our work can be seen as a response to the problem highlighted by Barczak et al. (2009) – namely, that translating insights from extant research in NPD to a practical setting may not always be feasible. The network-based methodology presented in this paper can be used by innovation managers to enhance organizational processes for identifying successful ideas; this is a natural practical benefit of methodological contributions in innovation research (Toubia & Netzer, 2017). For the empirical study, we implemented the methodology using a combination of standard software languages and programs, which can be integrated into an innovation department's existing analytics infrastructure with relative ease. Additionally, while we build on Goldenberg et al.'s intuition of idea components, our approach is fundamentally backward-looking. Rather than setting up the ideation problem as a mix-and-match exercise involving preexisting templates, our construction and interpretation of feature co-occurrence networks relies on looking back on ideas that have already been generated to extract insights for further ideation. The benefit of hindsight inherent to our approach may be especially useful for large organizations that are risk-averse or otherwise lack strong innovation capabilities (Lafley & Charan, 2008); it is also highly relevant to use cases in open innovation, where sifting through a large pool of existing ideas is a fundamental problem (Bayus, 2013; Chesbrough, Vanhaverbeke, & West, 2014). At the end of a large-scale idea competition, only a couple of the top-rated ideas typically make it to the next product development stage, while the remaining ideas are essentially thrown away. We show that taking a network perspective can allow innovation managers to extract value from the large body of ideas that do not end up winning in the competition. Lastly, we leverage a number of current advances in computing technology to enable the implementation of our network-based methodology and subsequent analyses. Echoing the thoughts of Varian (2014), we would argue that machine learning and data mining approaches showcased in our paper represent a significant untapped potential for innovation managers.

5.3 Implications for Future Research

The work presented in this paper can be extended in several ways due to the fundamental nature of the contributions. In general, it may be fruitful to refine and expand on the configurational view of ideas, extend the network-based methodology and validate it using more diverse empirical datasets. We would like to draw attention to two open questions that may represent particularly interesting avenues for future work.

The first open question relates to the fact that our approach to feature importance presented in this paper either considers each feature in isolation or as a member of the base/FNI feature groups. Yet, given N features, $C(N,k) = \frac{N!}{k!(N-k)!}$ possible k-tuples can be generated in general (e.g., feature pairs, triples and so on). The analysis of such feature tuples can potentially help expand our understanding of the idea DNA and its impact on the success of ideas. For example, which insights can be derived by identifying feature tuples that occur most often, and the proportion of these occurrences that are part of a successful idea? If we believe that only a small subset of feature combinations drive much of an idea's success outcome, we may expect to see a "long tail" in the frequency distribution of feature tuples. As in the case of feature-level analysis, we can generate tuple-level network measures and summarize these for inclusion in the between-idea classification model. Moreover, it is interesting to note that $\text{argmax}_k |C(N,k)| = \left\lceil \frac{N}{2} \right\rceil$, i.e., one can maximize the number of tuples generated for a fixed set of unique features of size N, by picking the size k of the tuple to be about half of N. This can intuitively be seen from the visual representation of Pascal's triangle. As k approaches $\left\lceil \frac{N}{2} \right\rceil$, we can think of our marginal information gain as increasing with each increment in k. Beyond $k = \left\lceil \frac{N}{2} \right\rceil$, picking a higher k no longer gives us additional tuples (i.e., data points) to generate network measures from. We thus may have a natural upper bound to the informational value gained from the tuple-level analysis.

The second open question concerns the relevance of the idea DNA theory and methodology to services as opposed to products. For example, Goldenberg et al. (1999) give an example of Domino's Pizza, highlighting the ability of the template method to cope with the difference between the features of the product (i.e., the pizza ingredients) and those of the fast-food service (e.g., aspects of the pizza delivery logistics). It may be worthwhile to empirically investigate the extent to which our notion of the idea DNA – namely the network of the idea's constituent features – can be used to identify winning ideas related to services. Moreover, in the idea competition data analyzed in this paper, each idea is represented by its textual description. The description of a service may be far more verbose, potentially taking the form of a contractual agreement or a business plan. An automated topic-modeling approach such as the LDA-based one we opted for in this paper may prove to be especially useful in mining complex texts to derive latent features of a service.

Appendix

A1. Sample Submission from Chocolate Idea Competition

Idea description: "*More than just words: The idea is to imprint different pre-defined slogans on the chunk rows. By this the tablet can be used as perfect little and but very nice present depending on the slogans topics e.g., birthday wishes; relationship anniversaries; as thank you to somebody; proof of friendship. I imagine this would be a nice moment to break the chunk row and hand this nice sentence over to the other person. An extension to this idea would be to offer a platform where consumers can upload proposals for slogans that might be used by the chocolate producer.*"

Average expert rating: 3.64

Average community rating: 4.32

A2. LDA Specifications for Feature Generation

In the paper, we focus on the 20 topic/10 word LDA specification. Here we present the outcomes of two alternative LDA specifications to show the effect of changing the number of topics and words.

Topics	Word 1	Word 2	Word 3	Word 4	Word 5
"Pieces"	chocolate	would	bar	one	piece
"White"	chocolate	would	bar	like	white
"Idea"	chocolate	idea	sweet	milk	taste
"Novelty"	chocolate	like	would	make	coconut
"Tasty"	chocolate	bar	milk	would	taste
"Sweetness"	chocolate	piece	would	alcohol	sweet
"Milk"	chocolate	would	could	like	milk
"Desire"	chocolate	bar	piece	one	would
"Creation"	chocolate	would	cheese	want	create
"Positivity"	chocolate	bar	milk	like	would

Table A2.1: Feature Generation for 10 Topics/5 Words LDA Specification

Topics	Word 1	Word 2	Word 3	Word 4	Word 5	Word 6	Word 7	Word 8	Word 9	Word 10
"Dark"	chocolate	bar	would	taste	dark	one	idea	milk	sweet	like
"Texture"	chocolate	milk	bar	white	would	one	crispy	black	dipped	make
"Look"	chocolate	bar	piece	would	like	could	different	one	milk	shape
"Possible"	chocolate	bar	would	could	milk	taste	4	cadbury	idea	2
"Novelty"	chocolate	bar	one	coconut	could	love	milk	form	idea	flavor
"Sharing"	chocolate	would	like	taste	white	fruit	cup	word	half	love
"Combining"	chocolate	bar	would	piece	one	like	taste	tea	also	milk
"Ingredients"	chocolate	like	would	milk	bar	cream	peanut	taste	new	ice
"Layering"	chocolate	bar	different	piece	one	melting	layer	milk	answer	gingerbread
"Summer"	chocolate	like	taste	could	icecream	want	make	flavor	bar	shape

Table A2.2: Feature Generation for 10 Topics/10 Words LDA Specification

A3. Descriptive Feature Statistics by LDA Specification

VARIABLES	Frequency of Occurrences across Ideas	
Base Features	**Absolute**	**Relative**
Pieces	193	41.2%
White	195	41.7%
Idea	237	50.6%
Novelty	218	46.6%
Tasty	208	44.4%
Sweetness	219	46.8%
Milk	212	45.3%
Desire	193	41.2%
Creation	253	54.1%
Positivity	195	41.7%
Feature Network Indices (FNIs)	**Mean**	**SD**
Average Weighted Degree	376.535	110.355
Unique Modularity Classes	1936	0.245
N = 468 ideas		

Table A3.1: Descriptive Statistics for 10 Topics/5 Words LDA Specification

VARIABLES	Frequency of Occurrences across Ideas	
Base Features	**Absolute**	**Relative**
Dark	208	44.4%
Texture	256	54.7%
Look	192	41.0%
Possible	212	45.3%
Novelty	229	48.9%
Sharing	240	51.3%
Combining	199	42.5%
Ingredients	198	42.3%
Layering	234	50.0%
Summer	211	45.1%
Feature Network Indices (FNIs)	**Mean**	**SD**
Average Weighted Degree	400.392	96.311
Unique Modularity Classes	2.573	0.537
N = 468 ideas		

Table A3.2: Descriptive Statistics for 10 Topics/10 Words LDA Specification

A4. Predictive Results

LDA Parameters	Predictors	Ratings (Chocolate Ideas)					
		Expert		Community		Combined	
		Actual Accuracy	Actual vs. Expected	Actual Accuracy	Actual vs. Expected	Actual Accuracy	Actual vs. Expected
10 Topics of 5 Words	Base	0.514	4.7%	0.505	-5.1%	0.514	-1.0%
	FNIs	0.477	-2.9%	0.510	-4.1%	0.477	-8.1%
	Base + FNIs	0.511	4.1%	0.497	-6.6%	0.511	-1.5%
10 Topics of 10 Words	Base	0.575	17.1%	0.525	-1.3%	0.575	10.8%
	FNIs	0.526	7.1%	0.520	-2.3%	0.526	1.3%
	Base + FNIs	0.567	15.5%	0.520	-2.3%	0.567	9.2%
20 Topics of 10 Words	Base	0.524	6.5%	0.560	5.3%	0.528	1.7%
	FNIs	0.513	4.5%	0.512	-3.8%	0.518	-0.2%
	Base + FNIs	0.528	7.4%	0.570	7.1%	0.537	3.5%
Expected Accuracy		**0.491**		**0.532**		**0.519**	

Notes:
Results are based on the roughly 37% out-of-bag sample of N = 468 ideas (i.e., about 172 unused observations per bootstrap sample)
Decimal values show mean actual predictive accuracy over 500 trees (all results significant at p < 0.01)
Percentage values show the computation *(Actual Accuracy / Expected Accuracy) - 1*
Expected accuracy is analogous to the proportion of successful ideas in the dataset

Table A4: Summary of Predictive Accuracies

A5. Variable Importance by Gini Index

Predictors: Base only	Importance using Gini Index	Jump in Importance	Predictors: Base + FNI	Importance using Gini Index	Jump in Importance
Summer	10.631	0.290	Average Degree Centrality	44.090	34.883
Shape	10.341	0.428	Summer	9.207	0.060
Nature	9.913	0.014	Game	9.147	0.559
Game	9.899	0.114	Shape	8.588	0.147
Nutty	9.786	0.057	Nature	8.441	0.163
Social	9.729	0.089	Social	8.278	0.512
Honey	9.640	0.256	Love	7.766	0.049
Sweet	9.384	0.023	Honey	7.717	0.008
Unique	9.361	0.026	Sweet	7.709	0.003
Love	9.335	0.021	Quantifiable	7.706	0.055
Pieces	9.314	0.004	Creation	7.652	0.155
Dark	9.310	0.226	Pieces	7.497	0.045
Layering	9.084	0.027	Dark	7.451	0.008
Creation	9.056	0.068	Health	7.443	0.039
Health	8.988	0.130	Layering	7.404	0.041
Fruity	8.859	0.303	Nutty	7.363	0.236
Quantifiable	8.556	0.337	Fruity	7.127	0.027
Novelty	8.219	0.083	Unique	7.101	0.188
Different	8.135	0.231	Novelty	6.913	0.360
Tasty	7.904	0.000	Different	6.554	0.540
			Tasty	6.014	4.047
			Unique Modularity Classes	1.967	0.000

Predictors: FNIs only	Importance using Gini Index	Jump in Importance
Average Degree Centrality	17.484	16.354
Unique Modularity Classes	1.130	1.130

Table A5: Variable Importance for 20 Topic/10 Words LDA Specification

A6. Probit Models for 20 Topics/10 Words LDA Specification

VARIABLES	Outcome: Expert Rating (success y/n)		
	Model 1 (Base only)	Model 2 (FNIs only)	Model 3 (Base + FNIs)
Summer	-0.059		-0.059
	[0.051]		[0.051]
Love	0.011		0.013
	[0.053]		[0.053]
Social	0.138**		0.135**
	[0.055]		[0.055]
Honey	-0.021		-0.029
	[0.053]		[0.055]
Creation	-0.000		-0.005
	[0.054]		[0.055]
Unique	-0.030		-0.035
	[0.056]		[0.057]
Nutty	0.139***		0.143***
	[0.054]		[0.054]
Quantifiable	-0.155***		-0.156***
	[0.056]		[0.056]
Pieces	0.053		0.049
	[0.053]		[0.054]
Nature	0.182***		0.184***
	[0.057]		[0.058]
Fruity	0.001		-0.002
	[0.056]		[0.056]
Tasty	0.070		0.069
	[0.062]		[0.062]
Sweet	0.001		-0.002
	[0.053]		[0.053]
Dark	0.003		-0.000
	[0.056]		[0.056]
Shape	0.035		0.033
	[0.051]		[0.051]
Health	-0.030		-0.031
	[0.054]		[0.054]
Layering	0.070		0.069
	[0.058]		[0.058]
Novelty	-0.077		-0.080
	[0.061]		[0.062]

Different	0.040		0.039
	[0.063]		[0.063]
Game	-0.125**		-0.129**
	[0.059]		[0.059]
Average Weighted Degree		0.000	(omitted)
		[0.000]	
Unique Modularity Classes		-0.083	0.055
		[0.096]	[0.099]
Wald X^2	46.05***	1.55	46.12***
Observations	468	468	468

Notes:
Coefficients show marginal effects of Probit regressions
Robust standard errors in brackets
*** p<0.01, ** p<0.05, * p<0.1

Table A6.1: Probit Models for Expert Rating Outcome

VARIABLES	Outcome: Community Rating (success y/n)		
	Model 1 (Base only)	Model 2 (FNIs only)	Model 3 (Base + FNIs)
Summer	0.040		0.040
	[0.051]		[0.051]
Love	0.047		0.048
	[0.055]		[0.055]
Social	0.145***		0.144***
	[0.055]		[0.056]
Honey	-0.077		-0.081
	[0.053]		[0.054]
Creation	-0.106**		-0.109**
	[0.053]		[0.054]
Unique	-0.020		-0.022
	[0.056]		[0.057]
Nutty	0.158***		0.161***
	[0.053]		[0.053]
Quantifiable	-0.124**		-0.125**
	[0.058]		[0.058]
Pieces	-0.057		-0.059
	[0.053]		[0.053]
Nature	-0.037		-0.036
	[0.058]		[0.058]
Fruity	0.072		0.071

	[0.058]		[0.058]
Tasty	0.020		0.020
	[0.063]		[0.063]
Sweet	-0.057		-0.059
	[0.054]		[0.055]
Dark	0.043		0.041
	[0.057]		[0.057]
Shape	0.096*		0.095*
	[0.051]		[0.051]
Health	-0.018		-0.019
	[0.055]		[0.055]
Layering	0.010		0.009
	[0.060]		[0.060]
Novelty	0.011		0.009
	[0.063]		[0.063]
Different	0.090		0.089
	[0.063]		[0.064]
Game	0.063		0.061
	[0.061]		[0.062]
Average Weighted Degree		0.000	
		[0.000]	
Unique Modularity Classes		-0.070	0.030
		[0.096]	[0.105]
Wald χ^2	30.45*	1.39	30.28*
Observations	468	468	468

Notes:
Coefficients show marginal effects of Probit regressions
Robust standard errors in brackets
*** $p<0.01$, ** $p<0.05$, * $p<0.1$

Table A6.2: Probit Models for Community Rating Outcome

VARIABLES	Outcome: Combined Rating (success y/n)		
	Model 1 (Base only)	Model 2 (FNIs only)	Model 3 (Base + FNIs)
Summer	-0.036		-0.036
	[0.051]		[0.051]
Love	0.089*		0.091*
	[0.054]		[0.054]
Social	0.122**		0.120**
	[0.056]		[0.057]
Honey	-0.017		-0.026
	[0.054]		[0.055]
Creation	-0.107**		-0.112**

	[0.054]		[0.055]
Unique	-0.006		-0.011
	[0.056]		[0.056]
Nutty	0.122**		0.126**
	[0.054]		[0.055]
Quantifiable	-0.111*		-0.113*
	[0.058]		[0.058]
Pieces	0.026		0.021
	[0.053]		[0.054]
Nature	0.097*		0.099*
	[0.058]		[0.058]
Fruity	0.009		0.006
	[0.057]		[0.057]
Tasty	0.002		0.001
	[0.064]		[0.064]
Sweet	-0.050		-0.053
	[0.054]		[0.054]
Dark	0.043		0.039
	[0.056]		[0.056]
Shape	0.105**		0.103**
	[0.051]		[0.051]
Health	-0.090*		-0.091*
	[0.054]		[0.054]
Layering	0.041		0.040
	[0.060]		[0.060]
Novelty	0.070		0.066
	[0.064]		[0.064]
Different	0.092		0.091
	[0.063]		[0.063]
Game	0.041		0.037
	[0.061]		[0.062]
Average Weighted Degree		0.000	
		[0.000]	
Unique Modularity Classes		-0.032	0.063
		[0.096]	[0.104]
Wald X^2	30.51*	2.14	30.38*
Observations	468	468	468

Notes:
Coefficients show marginal effects of Probit regressions
Robust standard errors in brackets
*** $p<0.01$, ** $p<0.05$, * $p<0.1$

Table A6.3: Probit Models for Combined Rating Outcome

A7. Linking Feature Uniqueness to Idea Success

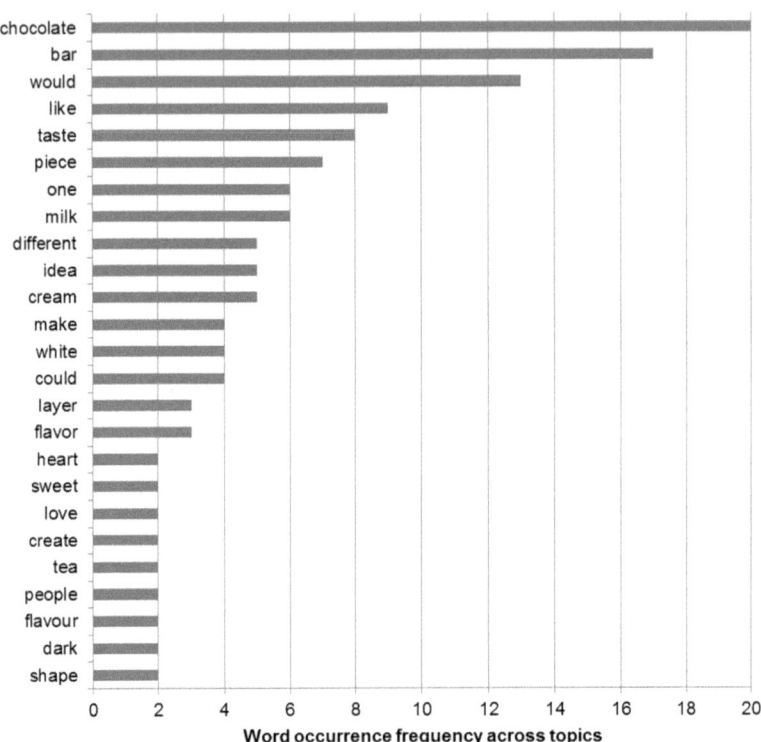

Figure A7: Most Common Words in 20 Topic/10 Words LDA Specification

	Ranking of topics by uniqueness when top N most common words considered			
Uniqueness	N = 5	N = 10	N = 20	N = 25
High (topic contains only 1-2 common words)	Quantifiable	Quantifiable	Quantifiable	Quantifiable
	Dark	Nature	Nature	Nature
	Nature	Dark	Social	Shape
	Social	Social	Health	Dark
	Health	Health	Nutty	Social
Medium (topic contains 2-5 common words)	Nutty	Shape	Shape	Health
	Love	Nutty	Dark	Nutty
	Shape	Love	Love	Creation
	Summer	Summer	Summer	Love
	Novelty	Novelty	Creation	Novelty
	Game	Game	Novelty	Game
	Creation	Creation	Game	Honey
Low (topic contains 5-10 common words)	Honey	Honey	Honey	Summer
	Unique	Fruity	Sweet	Unique
	Pieces	Tasty	Unique	Fruity
	Fruity	Sweet	Fruity	Tasty
	Tasty	Layering	Tasty	Sweet
	Sweet	Unique	Pieces	Pieces
	Layering	Pieces	Layering	Layering
	Different	Different	Different	Different

Note: Shaded topics are predictors with low importance based on Gini indices (Table A5) and Probit models (Tables A6.1-A6.3)

Table A7: Effect of Feature Uniqueness on Idea Success

A8. Formal Definitions of Network Measures

We describe the formalizations in terms of a network $G = (V, E)$ with $|V|$ nodes and $|E|$ edges. The network can equally be described by a weighted matrix W, such that the element W_{ij} represents the strength of the edge between nodes i and j (e.g., frequency of co-occurrences in the case of event data). Let the adjacency matrix A_{ij} denote a non-weighted version of W_{ij}, such that the element $A_{ij} = 1$ if nodes i and j are connected and 0 otherwise. Below are the typical definitions of network measures used in our paper (Newman, 2010; Opsahl, Agneessens, & Skvoretz, 2010; Wasserman & Faust, 1994):

- **Weighted Degree Centrality** $C_D{}^W$ of node i: $C_D{}^W(i) = \sum_j^{|V|} W_{ij}$
- **Modularity Class** c of node i: The modularity of a network partition is given by $Q = \frac{1}{2m} \sum_{i,j} \left[W_{ij} - \frac{k_i k_j}{2m} \right] \delta(c_i, c_j)$, where $k_i = \sum_j W_{ij}$, c_i is the modularity class (or network community/cluster) to which node i is assigned, $\delta(c_i, c_j) = 1$ if $c_i = c_j$ and 0 otherwise, and $m = \frac{1}{2} \sum_{ij} W_{ij}$.

References

Ahn, Y.-Y., Ahnert, S. E., Bagrow, J. P., & Barabási, A.-L. (2011). Flavor network and the principles of food pairing. *Scientific Reports, 1*.

Altshuller, G. S. (1984). *Creativity as an exact science: The theory of the solution of inventive problems*. New York: Gordon and Breach Science Publishers.

Archer, K. J., & Kimes, R. V. (2008). Empirical characterization of random forest variable importance measures. *Computational Statistics & Data Analysis, 52*(4), 2249–2260.

Barczak, G., Griffin, A., & Kahn, K. B. (2009). Perspective: trends and drivers of success in NPD practices: results of the 2003 PDMA best practices study. *Journal of Product Innovation Management, 26*(1), 3–23.

Bastian, M., Heymann, S., Jacomy, M., & others. (2009). Gephi: An open source software for exploring and manipulating networks. *ICWSM, 8*, 361–362.

Bayus, B. L. (2013). Crowdsourcing new product ideas over time: An analysis of the Dell IdeaStorm community. *Management Science, 59*(1), 226–244.

Beckman, S. L., & Barry, M. (2007). Innovation as a learning process: Embedding design thinking. *California Management Review, 50*(1), 25–56.

Björk, J., & Magnusson, M. (2009). Where do good innovation ideas come from? Exploring the influence of network connectivity on innovation idea quality. *Journal of Product Innovation Management, 26*(6), 662–670.

Blei, D. M., Ng, A. Y., & Jordan, M. I. (2003). Latent Dirichlet Allocation. *Journal of Machine Learning Research, 3*(1), 993–1022.

Blondel, V. D., Guillaume, J.-L., Lambiotte, R., & Lefebvre, E. (2008). Fast unfolding of communities in large networks. *Journal of Statistical Mechanics: Theory and Experiment, 2008*(10), P10008.

Breiman, L. (1996). Bagging predictors. *Machine Learning, 24*(2), 123–140.

Breiman, L. (2001). Random forests. *Machine Learning, 45*(1), 5–32.

Brown, B., & Anthony, S. D. (2011). How P&G tripled its innovation success rate. *Harvard Business Review, 89*(6), 64–72.

Chesbrough, H. W. (2003). *Open innovation: The new imperative for creating and profiting from technology*. Boston: Harvard Business School Press.

Chesbrough, H. W., Vanhaverbeke, W., & West, J. (2014). *New Frontiers in Open Innovation*. New York: Oxford University Press.

Cooper, R. G. (1988). Predevelopment activities determine new product success. *Industrial Marketing Management, 17*(3), 237–247.

Cooper, R. Easingwood, C. Edgett, S. Kleinschmidt, E. J. Storey, C. (1994). What distinguishes the top performing new products in financial services. *Journal of Product Innovation Management, 11*(4), 281–299.

Dahl, D. W., & Moreau, P. (2002). The influence and value of analogical thinking during new product ideation. *Journal of Marketing Research, 39*(1), 47–60.

Dhar, V., Geva, T., Oestreicher-Singer, G., & Sundararajan, A. (2014). Prediction in economic networks. *Information Systems Research, 25*(2), 264–284.

Dorst, K., & Cross, N. (2001). Creativity in the design process: co-evolution of problem-solution. *Design Studies, 22*(5), 425–437.

Dyer, J. H., Gregersen, H. B., & Christensen, C. M. (2009). The Innovator's DNA. *Harvard Business Review, 87*(12), 60–67.

Etzkowitz, H., & Leydesdorff, L. (2000). The dynamics of innovation: from National Systems and "Mode 2" to a Triple Helix of university-industry-government relations. *Research Policy, 29*(2), 109–123.

Fleming, L. (2001). Recombinant uncertainty in technological search. *Management Science, 47*(1), 117–132.

Gatignon, H., Tushman, M. L., Smith, W., & Anderson, P. (2002). A structural approach to assessing innovation: Construct development of innovation locus, type, and characteristics. *Management Science, 48*(9), 1103–1122.

Gavetti, G., & Rivkin, J. W. (2005). How strategists really think. *Harvard Business Review, 83*(4), 54–63.

Goldenberg, J., Lehmann, D. R., & Mazursky, D. (2001). The idea itself and the circumstances of its emergence as predictors of new product success. *Management Science, 47*(1), 69–84.

Goldenberg, J., & Mazursky, D. (1999). The voice of the product: Templates of new product emergence. *Creativity and Innovation Management, 8*(3), 157–164.

Goldenberg, J., Mazursky, D., & Solomon, S. (1999). Toward identifying the inventive templates of new products: A channeled ideation approach. *Journal of Marketing Research, 36*(2), 200–210.

Green, P. E., & Srinivasan, V. (2007). Conjoint analysis in consumer research: Issues and outlook. *Fundamentals of Marketing Research, 290–325.*

Green, P. E., & Srinivasan, V. (1978). Conjoint analysis in consumer research: issues and outlook. *Journal of Consumer Research, 5*(2), 103–123.

Haefliger, S., Krogh, G. von, & Spaeth, S. (2008). Code reuse in open source software. *Management Science, 54*(1), 180–193.

Hastie, T., Tibshirani, R., & Friedman J. (2009). *Elements of Statistical Learning* (2nd ed.): Springer.

Higgins, J. M. (1996). Innovate or evaporate: Creative techniques for strategists. *Long Range Planning, 29*(3), 370–380.

Huston, L., & Sakkab, N. (2006). Connect and develop. *Harvard Business Review, 84*(3), 58–66.

Jawecki, G., Gebauer, J., & Mathis-Alig, S. (2013). How Netnography Can Be Used to Unlock the Full Potential of Crowdsourcing Contests. *Esomar World Research*, 1–7.

Jerrard, B., Trueman, M., & Newport, R. (Eds.) 1999. *Managing new product innovation*. London: Taylor & Francis.

Koestler, A. (1989). *The Act of Creation*. London: Penguin Books.

Kornish, L. J., & Ulrich, K. T. (2011). Opportunity spaces in innovation: Empirical analysis of large samples of ideas. *Management Science, 57*(1), 107–128.

Kornish, L. J., & Ulrich, K. T. (2014). The importance of the raw idea in innovation: Testing the sow's ear hypothesis. *Journal of Marketing Research, 51*(1), 14–26.

Lafley, A. G., & Charan, R. (2008). *The game-changer: How you can drive revenue and profit growth with innovation*. New York: Crown Business.

Leung, A., Agarwal, A., Konana, P., & Kumar, A. (2016). Network Analysis of Search Dynamics: The Case of Stock Habitats. *Management Science, 63*(8), 2667–2687.

Liaw, A., & Wiener, M. (2002). Classification and regression by randomForest. *R News, 2*(3), 18–22.

Moreau, C. P., & Dahl, D. W. (2005). Designing the solution: The impact of constraints on consumers' creativity. *Journal of Consumer Research, 32*(1), 13–22.

Mueller, J. S., Melwani, S., & Goncalo, J. A. (2012). The bias against creativity: Why people desire but reject creative ideas. *Psychological Science, 23*(1), 13–17.

Newman, M. (2010). *Networks: An introduction*. New York: Oxford University Press.

Opsahl, T., Agneessens, F., & Skvoretz, J. (2010). Node centrality in weighted networks: Generalizing degree and shortest paths. *Social Networks, 32*(3), 245–251.

Perlich, C., Provost, F., & Simonoff, J. S. (2003). Tree induction vs. logistic regression: A learning-curve analysis. *Journal of Machine Learning Research, 4*(Jun), 211–255.

Pólya, G. (1971). *How to solve it: A new aspect of mathematical method* (2nd ed.). New Jersey: Princeton University Press.

Prahalad, C. K., & Ramaswamy, V. (2004a). *The future of competition: Co-creating unique value with customers*. Boston: Harvard Business Review Press.

Prahalad, C. K., & Ramaswamy, V. (2004b). Co-creation experiences: The next practice in value creation. *Journal of Interactive Marketing, 18*(3), 5–14.

Rietzschel, E. F., Nijstad, B. A., & Stroebe, W. (2006). Productivity is not enough: A comparison of interactive and nominal brainstorming groups on idea generation and selection. *Journal of Experimental Social Psychology, 42*(2), 244–251.

Rietzschel, E. F., Nijstad, B. A., & Stroebe, W. (2010). The selection of creative ideas after individual idea generation: choosing between creativity and impact. *British Journal of Psychology, 101*(1), 47–68.

Rogers, E. M. (2003). *Diffusion of Innovations* (5th ed.). New York: Free Press.

Scott, J. (2012). *Social Network Analysis* (3rd ed.). London: Sage.

Sommer, S. C., & Loch, C. H. (2004). Selectionism and learning in projects with complexity and unforeseeable uncertainty. *Management Science, 50*(10), 1334–1347.

Teng, C.-Y., Lin, Y.-R., & Adamic, L. A. (2012). Recipe recommendation using ingredient networks. In *Proceedings of the 4th Annual ACM Web Science Conference* (pp. 298–307).

Terwiesch, C., & Ulrich, K. T. (2009). *Innovation tournaments: Creating and selecting exceptional opportunities*. Boston: Harvard Business Press.

Toubia, O., & Florès, L. (2007). Adaptive idea screening using consumers. *Marketing Science, 26*(3), 342–360.

Toubia, O., & Netzer, O. (2017). Idea Generation, Creativity, and Prototypicality. *Marketing Science, 36*(1), 1–20.

Trott, P. (2012). *Innovation management and new product development* (5th ed.). New York: Prentice Hall.

Varian, H. R. (2014). Big data: New tricks for econometrics. *The Journal of Economic Perspectives, 28*(2), 3–27.

Wasserman, S., & Faust, K. (1994). *Social Network Analysis: Methods and Applications* (Vol. 8): Cambridge University Press.

Wenger, E. C., & Snyder, W. M. (2000). Communities of practice: The organizational frontier. *Harvard Business Review, 78*(1), 139–146.

Essay 3:

Dynamic Pricing of New Products - The Effects of Strategic Momentum and Feature Composition

Chinmay Kakatkar and Martin Spann

Abstract

In the context of new product development (NPD), setting a pricing strategy for newly launched products is a clear challenge for firms. Setting the starting price too low may forego the value from customers with a higher willingness to pay (e.g., early adopters), while setting the price too high may make it difficult for product adoption to take off. Extant literature suggests that dynamic pricing strategies may be defined in terms of the introductory price and the subsequent pricing trajectory of the product with respect to the market. Whereas past research has considered firm-level and market-level correlates of dynamic pricing strategies, we focus on correlates of pricing that arise from the product itself. Specifically, we investigate the correlational effects of strategic momentum (i.e., whether a new product's pricing strategy matches that of its predecessor in a product series) and feature composition (in terms feature breadth and the "core-ness" of features in a product). Findings based on a study of the market for new cameras suggest that the predecessor's pricing strategy and measures of feature composition can be viable correlates of the new product's pricing strategy. Our method and findings offer interesting insights for scholars and practitioners by providing a more nuanced understanding of the link between a product's characteristics and the related pricing strategies.

Keywords: Dynamic Pricing, Network Analysis, New Product Development, Product Features, Strategic Momentum

1. Introduction

When Apple brought the first iPhone to market, the initial unit price was set as high as 599 USD (Kotler & Armstrong, 2014, p. 336). By contrast, Samsung has been known for introducing smartphones at more competitive price points. As their products mature and progress through their respective lifecycles, these companies tend to either fight to keep a product's price roughly constant or even raise them (e.g., by driving up the consumers' perceived value of the product via indirect network effects of accessories) (Liu, 2010), or lower them in the face of rising competition and improvements in technology (Bayus, 1992). In the context of new product development (NPD), pricing is a clear challenge for firms. Setting the starting price too low may "leave money on the table", especially given customers with a higher willingness to pay (e.g., early adopters), while setting the price too high may make it difficult for product adoption to take off (Golder & Tellis, 2004). Firms can choose from a variety of dynamic pricing strategies for new products (Tellis, 1986), and two approaches in particular have crystallized over the past few decades of marketing research (Dean, 1976; Nagle, Zale, & Hogan, 2011; Tellis, 1986): skimming and penetration.

The normative pricing literature suggests that skimming and penetration represent two fundamentally contrasting views of tackling the pricing challenge of NPD. A firm employing price skimming (e.g., Apple) would set the introductory product price above the average market price for the product's feature bundle, with the aim of exploiting customer heterogeneity and capturing the demand at the higher price points when the demand is fairly price inelastic (Dean, 1976; Tellis, 1986). Meanwhile, a firm using penetration pricing (e.g., Samsung) would set this price below the market price, essentially foregoing some early profit in the interest of capturing more of the market share (Kotler & Armstrong, 2014, p. 337). Spann, Fischer, and Tellis (2015) differentiate between such dynamic pricing strategies based on the initial price (below, above or at the average market price of a product's feature bundle) and its subsequent trajectory (decreasing, increasing or staying with the market trajectory); the authors classify the resulting nine pricing strategies in a manner that is consistent with Nagle et al. (2011, p. 125). Interestingly, in their empirical analysis of the market for new digital cameras, Spann et al. (2015) observe only five of the nine possible strategies. The focus of the authors was to classify as well as analyze the prevalence and correlates of dynamic pricing strategies in the market for digital cameras. In this paper, we take the five resulting pricing strategies as outcome variables and set out to identify two sets of possible correlates that might stem from the product itself.

First, we consider the relationship of the product's pricing strategy with respect to that of its predecessor. Note that our view of product succession in this paper is restricted to incremental innovation within a given "product line" or "product series" (Gatignon, Tushman, Smith, & Anderson, 2002). In the digital camera market, for example, "PowerShot" and "Digital IXUS" are two different product series of the camera maker Canon; the camera model "PowerShot A 20", introduced in an earlier time period and containing older technology, may be considered a predecessor of the "PowerShot A 30". Now, a firm may choose to replicate the previous product's pricing strategy or switch to a different strategy (Bayus, 1992). Borrowing terminology from the finance literature, we refer to the underlying phenomenon as "strategic momentum", in the sense that a firm may stick with the previous type of strategy ("momentum continual") or change it ("momentum reversal") (Cooper, Gutierrez, & Hameed, 2004).

Second, we look at the association between a product's feature composition and pricing strategy. Following Spann et al. (2015), we assume that heterogeneous products can be seen as an aggregation (i.e., bundle) of their constituent features. For technology products like cameras, the features are typically listed in detail in the product's technical specification or a similar document. Previous research has suggested that a product's features can be segmented into core and peripheral features (Tushman & Murmann, 1998). Interestingly, the literature distinguishes between these feature segments in terms of the features' "centrality", which strongly evokes terminology commonly used in network analysis (Newman, 2010). Building on this intuition, we conceptualize a product as a network of its constituent features and use well-known centrality measures (degree and betweenness centrality) to identify core and peripheral features. Furthermore, we employ network clustering analysis to operationalize the notion of feature breadth in terms of the number of different feature types contained in a given product.

To what extent do strategic momentum and feature composition correlate with a product's dynamic pricing strategy? We address this overarching research question by empirically analyzing the whole market for digital cameras in one major European country for 46 months, and obtain four main findings. In line with our theoretical expectations, we find that the use of a downward pricing trajectory for the predecessor is correlated with a downward pricing trajectory for the next product in the series, reflecting a continual of the strategic pricing momentum. An upward pricing trajectory for the predecessor is also correlated with a downward pricing trajectory for the next product, which can be plausibly explained based on the high intensity of competition in the market. The two findings related to feature composition are somewhat more surprising. Decreasing the share of peripheral features and the feature breadth for the new product appears to be associated with pricing strategies that set the initial price at or above the market and have an upward trajectory. By contrast, increasing peripheral features and feature breadth is closely linked to pricing strategies where the price starts below the market and continues on a downward trajectory. We reconcile these results via previous empirical research on feature fatigue and the use of pricing as a means of "testing the waters" in NPD. Ultimately, we aim at contributing to the literature on the dynamic pricing of new products. The results can help firms analyze the strategic behavior of competitors, as well as giving market analysts and policy makers insights into the pricing decisions of firms regarding technology product lines. Scholars and practitioners can also apply the network methodology described in this paper to analyze the feature composition of new products.

The remainder of the paper is organized as follows. Section 2 draws on related literature to derive hypotheses for the effects of strategic momentum and feature composition on the choice of dynamic pricing strategies for new products. Section 3 describes the process of augmenting the camera dataset used by Spann et al. (2015) to construct new variables of interest. Section 4 tests our hypotheses by analyzing the augmented data. Finally, Section 5 ends with a conclusion and discussion of our findings.

2. Theory and Hypotheses

The five pricing strategies observed empirically by Spann et al. (2015) in their analysis of the market for new cameras are depicted in Figure 1 (both product price and product age in terms of life cycle time are log-scaled). Three of the strategies exhibit a downward trajectory (D1, D2 and D3), while the remaining two have an upward trajectory (U1 and U2); beyond the directionality of the lines, the magnitude of their slopes are purely illustrative relative to each other.

D1 represents the path of the market price, which serves as a baseline for understanding the other strategies. The market price is defined as the average price consumers pay for a product given its bundle of features (Spann et al., 2015). Extant literature provides an economic rationale for the downward trend of market pricing from the perspective of sellers and consumers. As the various players in the supply chain produce more units of the product, they can move further down the experience curve and may develop more cost-effective ways of delivering the product at the required level of quality (Adler & Clark, 1991; Kalish, 1983). In a competitive industry with price-conscious consumers, incumbents may follow a downward pricing trajectory to combat existing competitors and the threat of new entrants

(Porter, 1979). Consumers may also be willing to wait for lower prices and possibly even leapfrog intermediate product versions in the case of products such as consumer electronics that are characterized by a rapid pace of innovation (Mohr, Sengupta, & Slater, 2010).

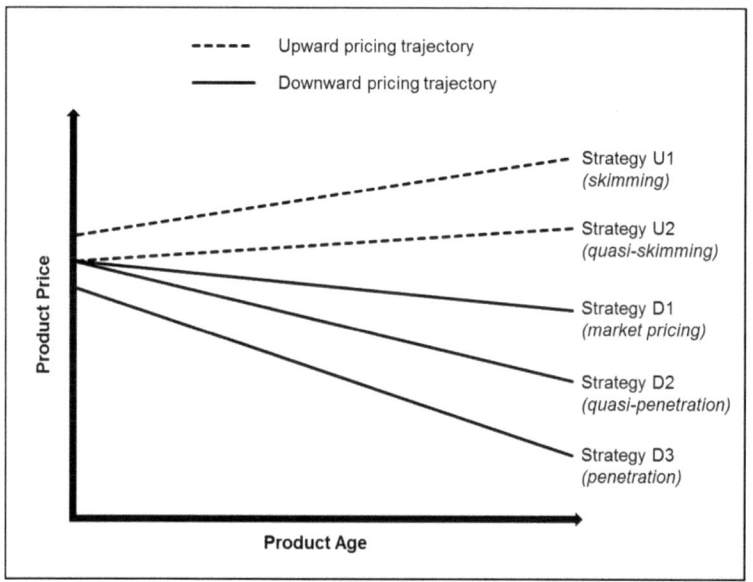

Figure 1: Pricing Strategies on Log-Log Scale

In line with the notion of penetration pricing, strategy D3 sets the introductory price of the product below the market price with the aim of penetrating the mass market from the start. As Dean (1976) notes, the low-price entry may be justifiable if the short-run demand for the product is price-elastic, if economies of production can be generated, and the firm faces a high level of competition. Similarly, Spann et al. (2015) suggest that penetration pricing may be correlated with competitive intensity, a later market stage (Golder & Tellis, 2004), and the producer's cumulative sales volume (Monroe, 2003). Strategy D2 is essentially a milder version of D3 in that it starts off at the market price but pulls away from it over time. We thus refer to D2 as a "quasi-penetration" strategy to differentiate it from D3. As with market pricing, the downward trend of D2 and D3 can be explained in terms of learning effects of the producer and the formulation of price-related expectations of the consumer.

Meanwhile, a firm using price skimming can set the introductory price above the market (e.g., as in U1) in certain conditions, such as if demand is price-inelastic, large enough segments of consumers with a high willingness to pay exist, if the firm is in a position to leverage its high reputation to demand higher prices, or if the firm is forced to attempt price skimming in order to recoup high start-up costs (e.g., of R&D and promotion) (Dean, 1976). Yet, competitive forces can compel the firm to bring the initially high product price in line with the market or even go below it (Porter, 1979). A skimming strategy with a downward trajectory could take advantage of the distribution of reservation prices of a heterogeneous consumer base and aim to capture more of the consumer surplus (Kotler & Armstrong, 2014, p. 336; Tellis, 1986). The rationale for skimming strategies with upward trajectories is somewhat different. Spann et al. (2015) suggest that a firm with a high brand reputation, high distribution strength and broad product line may opt for pricing strategies like U1 (skimming from the start) and U2 ("quasi-skimming", i.e., starting with the market price but then moving above it over time). In essence, the upward trajectory may be feasible when the firm is so powerful that it can "get away with it" (e.g., a monopolist) or can convince consumers that higher prices reflect the product's superior value, even in a competitive industry like consumer electronics (Dean, 1976; Nagle et al., 2011, p. 126).

2.1 Strategic Momentum

Suppose that a firm is about to launch the next product in a given series. In deciding the pricing strategy for this new product, the firm can choose from three broad options in relation to the strategy used for the predecessor: (1) use the same strategy, (2) use a strategy with the same trajectory, and (3) use a strategy with a different trajectory. Options 1 and 2 entail a continual of the strategic momentum in terms of the pricing trajectory, while option 3 reflects a reversal in momentum. To what extent does the choice of options 1, 2 or 3 for the new product correlate with the pricing strategy of the predecessor in a market such as the one for cameras studied by Spann et al. (2015)? We argue that the correlation between the trajectories of the past and present pricing strategies can be explained using a consumer-oriented reference price argument in the context of a competitive market.

Kalyanaram and Winer (1995) define a consumer's reference price as an "internal standard against which observed prices are compared". The firm, in its effort to match demand, will try to influence and match the final reference price of consumers at any given point in order to make the sale (Mazumdar, Raj, & Sinha, 2005). The formulation of an internal standard or benchmark about a product implies both a temporal and a contextual component (Rajendran & Tellis, 1994).

The temporal component captures the process of learning from past information (e.g., by having used a similar product before). The contextual component captures the tendency of consumers to compare products with a certain context (e.g., products in the same product category, of the same brand, sold in the same store). Using the temporal and contextual information, a consumer may set an expectation about the price of the new product (i.e., a reference price); note that the variety of factors affecting and distorting a consumer's perception of a "fair" price inherently makes the formulation of a reference price an exercise in approximation under uncertainty (Bolton, Warlop, & Alba, 2003; Thaler, 1985).

Arguably, the logic of reference price formulation can be applied to the case of a consumer forming an expectation about a product's pricing trajectory. Based on temporal and contextual information, for example, a consumer looking to purchase the next product in a series may expect the seller to set the introductory price above the market and then reduce the price over time; this would reflect an expectation of a strategy of skimming in the sense of periodic discounting (Tellis, 1986). Indeed, by extending this line of reasoning, a consumer would expect the firm to use the same pricing strategy for all comparable products (e.g., those in a given product series). Since firms will ultimately shape and match the consumers' expectations, it would seem that the strategy used for a predecessor should perfectly predict the strategy for a new product. However, the above reasoning does not yet consider the effect of competition on a firm's pricing policy. A firm may, for example, wish to try differentiating itself from its competitors along a dimension such as quality (Kotler & Armstrong, 2014, p. 557), and thus temporarily implement pricing strategies with an above-market introductory price and/or an upward trajectory for a given product. Note that, by definition, the market price itself would also increase if "better" features are added to a product's feature bundle. Thus, setting a product's price above the market price implies that the effect of the "better" features on the given product is disproportionately higher than the market expectation. Yet, in markets with high competitive intensity, such a skimming strategy may not be sustainable for future products in the series, as reference prices – potentially reinforced through improvements in production efficiency, and trends in technological obsolescence – conspire to pull prices down (Bayus, 1992; Spann et al., 2015). This leads to the following two hypotheses about strategic momentum:

- **H1:** The use of a pricing strategy with a *downward trajectory* (i.e., D1-D3) for a predecessor is **(a)** positively correlated with the use of the same type of strategy, and **(b)** negatively correlated with upward pricing trajectories (U1-U2), for the new product (i.e., momentum continual).

- **H2:** The use of a pricing strategy with an *upward trajectory* (i.e., U1-U2) for a predecessor is **(a)** positively correlated with the use of a downward pricing strategy (D1-D3), and **(b)** negatively correlated with the use of the same type of strategy, for the new product (i.e., momentum reversal).

2.2 Feature Composition

The pricing strategy may also be associated with the evolution of the product itself. Extant literature related to patterns of innovation and NPD suggests that variables at the level of the firm or the market give an incomplete account of a product's evolution; to get the full picture, it may be necessary to consider the nature and composition of the product features as well (Abernathy & Utterback, 1978; Anderson & Tushman, 1990). While the seminal research on dominant designs in innovation took the product as the primary unit of analysis (Abernathy & Utterback, 1978; Tushman & Anderson, 1986), later work has developed a more complex conceptualization of products as systems of interdependent features (Christensen, Suárez, & Utterback, 1998; Murmann & Frenken, 2006; Tushman & Murmann, 1998).

Taking the view of products as being composed of "nested hierarchies of subsystems and linking mechanisms", Gatignon et al. (2002) suggest that a product may be segmented into core and peripheral features. Core features are tightly coupled to other features, and their strong association to the dominant design implies that core features may persist through multiple innovations of the product series (Tushman & Murmann, 1998). Peripheral features are strategically more detached from the rest of the product, and may be more freely added or removed in successive product releases. For example, the pixel resolution and zoom would likely be core features of a camera, while card slots and connectivity ports may be more peripheral to the product function. An implication of the dichotomy of core and peripheral features for NPD is the need to balance the feature composition in a manner that ensures the maintainability and extensibility of the underlying product architecture (Ulrich & Eppinger, 2015, pp. 185–205). In particular, since such considerations could feed into the managerial decisions that contribute to the evolution of the new product, they may also be correlated with the product's pricing strategy.

Interestingly, the language used to describe core and peripheral features tends to evoke the concept of centrality in network analysis. For instance, Tushman and Murmann (1998) observe that product features may vary in their degree of centrality, suggesting that a product may indeed be viewed as a network of interconnected features of varying importance. As illustrated in Figure 2, each node in a product network conceptually represents a feature, and two nodes are connected by an edge if their corresponding features co-occur in a product; the frequency of co-occurrence of a feature pair is reflected by the edge weight (line thickness).

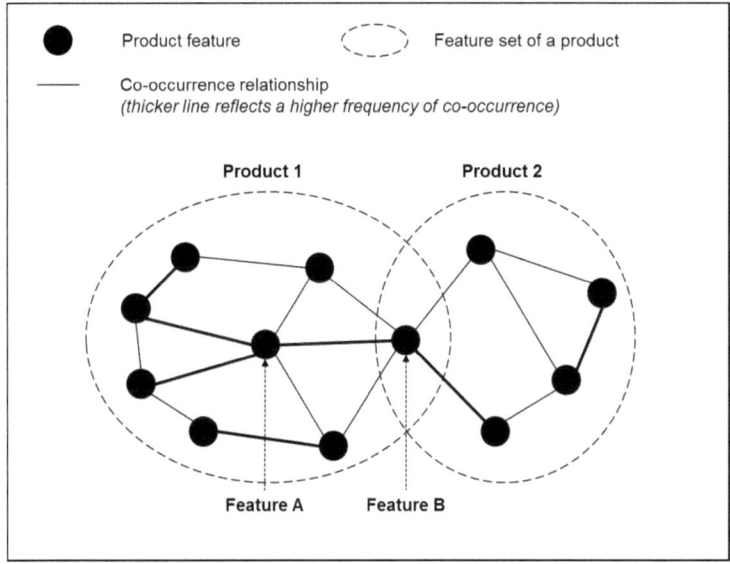

Figure 2: Products as Network of Features

Weighted degree and betweenness are two network-based measures of centrality that seem particularly relevant to the concept of feature "core-ness" (Newman, 2010, pp. 168–185). The weighted degree centrality of a feature is a function of the number of other features it co-occurs with across products, and the frequency of those co-occurrences. For instance, feature A in Figure 2 has a relatively high weighted degree centrality. Betweenness centrality captures a different notion of feature importance; features with a high betweenness represent a potential bridge between features from different clusters in the network (Newman, 2005). In Figure 2, feature B has a relatively high betweenness centrality since it bridges the feature clusters that happen to be associated with products 1 and 2. Moreover, the concept of the feature network also yields at least two measures of feature breadth, namely the number of features in the network, and the number of sub-product feature communities (Blondel, Guillaume, Lambiotte, & Lefebvre, 2008; Newman, 2010, p. 229). A higher feature breadth might reflect product richness, appeal to different user groups, or a firm's desire to experiment (Ulrich & Eppinger, 2015). The formal definitions of the network measures used in this paper are provided in Appendix A1.

To what extent does the feature composition of a product correlate with its pricing strategy? Let us first consider the case of upward pricing trajectories (i.e., strategies U1-U2 in Figure 1). Based on the earlier discussion, a firm's decision to price the product above the market price can signal a differentiation strategy and a higher valuation by the consumer (Monroe, 2003; Nagle et al., 2011). However, past research has shown that a consumer's ability to evaluate products (and map value to price) is inherently bounded by a number of factors, such as experience, retail context and personality traits (Bolton et al., 2003; Moreau, Lehmann, & Markman, 2001). One typical approach that firms and consumers may take in resolving the issue of evaluating product value is to focus on "add-ons", i.e., peripheral features (Ellison, 2005; Guiltinan, 1987). By adding peripheral features to a relatively stable set of core features, firms can construct a variety of different products, and thus potentially follow a strategy of feature-based price discrimination (Ellison, 2005).

New peripheral features may be less well-understood by consumers than core features, and the link between peripherals and the product's price may even be obscured by the firm (Gabaix & Laibson, 2006). Yet, studies have shown that peripherals can affect a consumer's evaluation of a product's appeal (Bertini, Ofek, & Ariely, 2009; Wathieu & Bertini, 2007). More features (especially peripheral "bells and whistles") may also confer social utility to consumers in terms of conspicuous consumption, justifying an above-market pricing strategy (Chaudhuri & Majumdar, 2006; Thompson & Norton, 2011). For later products in a larger series, a consumer may see additional value in peripherals if they help her to potentially recoup the sunk costs of owning/using a predecessor (Gill, 2008); this may partly explain the appeal of peripheral connectivity ports and other accessories for technology products. The implication of such a "more is better" view is that an increase in the feature breadth and share of peripherals in a product's feature set should be positively correlated with an upward-oriented pricing strategy. This leads to our first hypothesis about feature composition:

- **H3:** An increase in **(a)** peripheral features and **(b)** feature breadth will be positively correlated with upward pricing trajectories (U1-U2) for the new product.

Now let us consider the case of the downward pricing trajectories shown in Figure 1 (D1-D3). Downward trajectories such as those of market and penetration pricing may be associated with tougher competition, later market entry, and a more price-conscious consumer base (Golder & Tellis, 2004; Spann et al., 2015; Tellis, 1986). It would therefore seem reasonable to expect the products following strategies D1-D3 to be geared more towards mainstream and late-adopting consumers (Mohr et al., 2010). Crucially, based on the above rationale, these consumers are likely to see limited value in – and thus be less willing to pay for – peripherals and feature breadth, since they may lack the understanding and/or desire to exploit the feature richness across various use cases (Mukherjee & Hoyer, 2001; Simonson, Carmon, & O'Curry, 1994). The aversion to certain (peripheral) features may be especially strong, if they have not been valued positively in a previous product (Meyer, Zhao, & Han, 2008), or if they are seen as unnecessarily increasing product complexity (Moffatt, Sitzia, & Zizzo, 2015; Mukherjee & Hoyer, 2001; Sonsino, Benzion, & Mador, 2002). Thus, from the firm's perspective, it could make more economic sense to take a "back to the basics" approach to NPD, sticking close to the core feature set required by the dominant design, and minimizing peripheral embellishments. This leads to our second hypothesis about feature composition:

- **H4:** A decrease in **(a)** peripheral features and **(b)** feature breadth will be positively correlated with downward pricing trajectories (D1-D3) for the new product.

3. Empirical Study

3.1 Data

We use the camera dataset first presented by Spann et al. (2015). The data encompasses the whole market for digital cameras in one major European country over a period of 46 months, from January 2000 to October 2003. The data includes all market introductions of new cameras, product features, retail prices and sales. Further, we use the pricing strategy of each camera as identified by Spann et al. In particular, we are concerned with using and/or constructing five types of variables: (1) the pricing strategy used for a new camera model, (2) the pricing strategy used for the said camera model's predecessor, (3) the core-ness and (4) breadth of a given camera model's features, and (5) other controls. Table 1 shows the descriptive statistics for all of the variables in our augmented dataset, and we describe their derivation in the following.

While the pricing strategy for each new camera model (i.e., the outcome variable of our analysis) is available from the dataset produced by Spann et al., the strategy of each camera model's predecessor is not. This requires extending the existing dataset with a many-to-one mapping of camera models to series. However, a firm can introduce multiple camera models of the same series in a given time period, such that a new camera may in turn have multiple immediate predecessors; this is problematic for us, since we would like to have a single value for the predecessor's pricing strategy. We resolve this problem by considering the mode strategy of the potentially multiple immediate predecessors as our single-value variable for the predecessor's pricing strategy. The economic rationale for taking the mode is that, although a firm may choose to take a portfolio approach to diversify its pricing strategies across multiple same-period product introductions, the mode roughly captures the firm's dominant strategic position (Krishnan & Ulrich, 2001; Noble & Gruca, 1999). The top portion of Table 1 shows the descriptive statistics for the pricing strategy variables, and also shows aggregate variables for pricing trajectories. For instance, on average, 33% of the new camera models in our data follow an upward pricing trajectory, of which strategy U1 (skimming) accounts for 21.3% and U2 (quasi-skimming) accounts for 11.7%. It is also worth noting that, while the dataset used by Spann et al. (2015) contains 663 different camera models, only 367 have an observed predecessor and can therefore be used in our analysis.

Next, we derive variables representing the core-ness and breadth of a given camera model's feature set. The features cover the camera's pixel resolution, optical and digital zoom, ports and card slots, and other add-ons (e.g., MP3 player, Bluetooth connectivity). Descriptions of the full set of binary features that we use are provided in Appendix A2. To get from this model-level feature data to the kind of feature network conceptually depicted in Figure 2, we proceed as follows. We begin by constructing a co-occurrence matrix M, in which an element m_{ij} denotes the number of times features i and j both occur in the same product. Now, M yields a feature network of nodes (features) and edges (co-occurrence relationships) as required. Most of the feature variables in the original dataset are binary (1 = present, 0 = not present in the camera model), so for the sake of consistency, we dichotomize the three features that are not – pixel resolution (split into 500-pixel buckets), optical and digital zoom factor (split into categorical dummies).

We take the network measures of weighted degree and betweenness as proxies for a feature's core-ness. We first compute the mean weighted degree and betweenness of the full feature set, and then dichotomize the "core-ness" of all features around these mean values. For example, if a feature has an above-average weighted degree then this feature is considered "core" in terms of weighted degree. We can thus compute the share of core and peripheral features per camera model by the two network measures of centrality. Moreover, a camera model that has several features – and whose features belong to several different network clusters – can be said to have a high feature breadth. We generate feature clusters using the modularity-based community detection method developed by Blondel et al. (2008). Our generation of the co-occurrence matrix M and the derivation of network measures are automated using Python and the software tool Gephi (Bastian, Heymann, & Jacomy, 2009).

VARIABLES	N	Mean	SD	Min	Max
Outcome (Pricing strategy of new product)					
Upward Pricing Trajectory (U1 & U2)	367	0.330	0.471	0.000	1.000
U1: Skimming	367	0.213	0.410	0.000	1.000
U2: Quasi-skimming	367	0.117	0.322	0.000	1.000
D1: Market-pricing	367	0.373	0.484	0.000	1.000
D2: Quasi-penetration	367	0.079	0.270	0.000	1.000
D3: Penetration	367	0.218	0.413	0.000	1.000
Correlates					
Pricing strategy of predecessor					
Upward pricing trajectory (U1 & U2)	367	0.420	0.494	0.000	1.000
U1: Skimming	367	0.150	0.357	0.000	1.000
U2: Quasi-skimming	367	0.270	0.444	0.000	1.000
D1: Market-pricing	367	0.147	0.355	0.000	1.000
D2: Quasi-penetration	367	0.226	0.419	0.000	1.000
D3: Penetration	367	0.207	0.406	0.000	1.000
Feature core-ness					
Weighted degree centrality	367	0.814	0.119	0.500	1.000
Betweenness centrality	367	0.793	0.096	0.556	1.000
Feature breadth					
Number of product features	367	8.469	2.210	3.000	11.000
Number of feature clusters	367	4.578	1.507	1.000	6.000
Controls					
Introduction period (in months, 1 = Jan 2000)	367	28.390	11.445	1.000	43.000
Post market takeoff (1 = yes)	367	0.700	0.459	0.000	1.000
Mean introductory price (in EUR)	367	419.419	327.923	23.233	2220.700

Table 1: Descriptive Statistics of Augmented Camera Dataset

Finally, in line with the reasoning provided by Spann et al. (2015), we consider three control variables: the period in which a new camera model is introduced, whether this introduction period is before or after the market take-off point and the introductory product price; takeoff is identified by using the threshold rule from Golder and Tellis (1997). A later introduction period may be more correlated with market pricing (Bowman & Gatignon, 1996; Carpenter & Nakamoto, 1989), entry after the market take-off point may correlate with penetration pricing (Golder & Tellis, 2004), and a higher introductory price could indicate a tendency towards skimming (Tellis, 1986).

3.2 Descriptive Analysis

The overall descriptive statistics shown in Table 1 reflect some interesting aspects of our augmented camera dataset. As observed by Spann et al. (2015), firms tend to use market pricing for new camera models, and this mainly drives the percentage of downward pricing strategies (D1-D3) in the data.

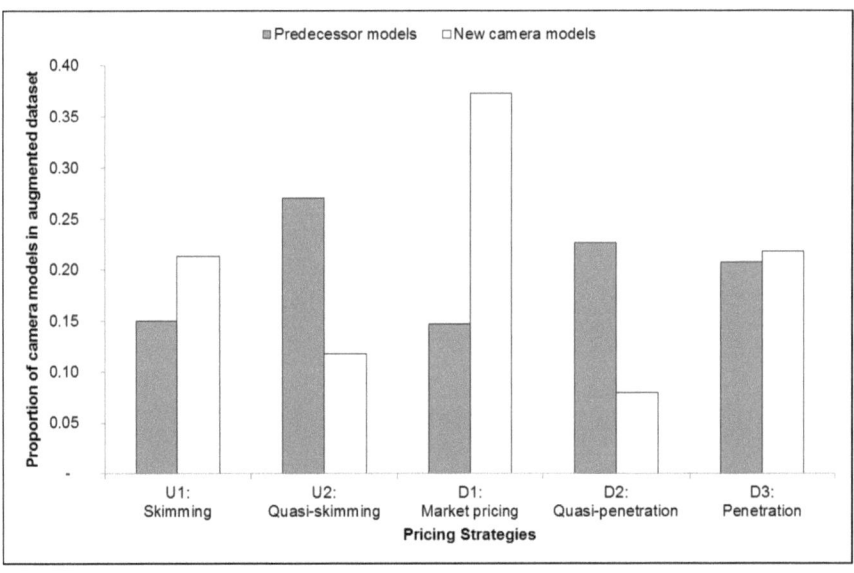

Figure 3: Distribution of Pricing Strategies in New and Predecessor Camera Models

However, the distributions of pricing strategies for new and predecessor camera models are evidently quite different, as shown in Figure 3, and appear to be in line with our empirical assumptions drawn from Spann et al. (2015). For instance, we assume order-of-entry effects based on extant literature, and thus expect late entrants to use mainly market pricing. One implication of this assumption is that a new model is more likely to follow market pricing than its predecessor, as seen in Figure

3. The strategy distributions for predecessors and new models tend to remain relatively unchanged for the extreme/pure strategies (U1, D3), while the camera product lines following the quasi/impure strategies (U2, D2) appear to converge to market pricing (D1) for the new models.

Moreover, the share of core features per product is subtly different based on the measure of core-ness we consider. Based on the mean statistics in Table 1, about 80% of the features in a given camera model can be considered core. Yet, as Figure 4 shows, the distribution of the core-ness by the weighted degree centrality measure somewhat approximates a (normal) bell curve, while core-ness by the betweenness measure exhibits some kurtosis. Similarly, jointly tabulating the two measures of feature breadth (i.e., number of product features and feature clusters) in Table 2 provides additional information to their descriptive interpretation. For example, most camera models appear to consist of about 10 features that belong to 5-6 clusters.

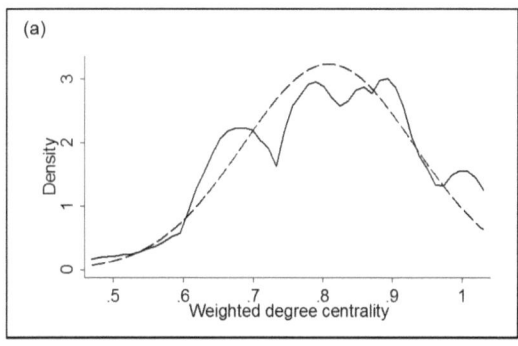

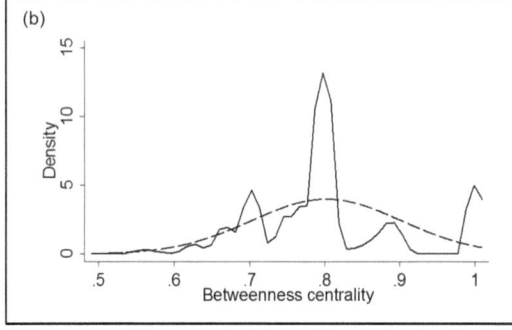

Figure 4: Distributions of Feature Core-ness Correlates (dashed line is normal curve)

Number of product features	Number of feature clusters						Total
	1	2	3	4	5	6	
3	22	1	0	0	0	0	23
4	4	13	2	0	0	0	19
5	0	12	3	0	0	0	15
6	0	0	2	3	0	0	5
7	0	0	9	9	0	0	18
8	0	0	5	20	11	1	37
9	0	0	0	14	37	17	68
10	0	0	0	1	80	97	178
11	0	0	0	0	3	1	4
Total	26	26	21	47	131	116	367

Table 2: Distribution of Feature Breath Correlates

3.3 Regression Results

In this paper we use the standard Probit specification with robust standard errors (as implemented in Stata 13) to estimate the effects of strategic momentum and feature composition as correlates of a new camera model's pricing strategy. Note that we are not primarily interested in maximizing the predictive accuracy of the correlates, so we avoid using related methods more common in the domain of machine learning (Varian, 2014). By using the Probit instead, we aim to test the hypotheses presented in Section 2 in a traditional way that is familiar to fellow marketing and innovation scholars.

Table 3 presents the full specifications for each of the binary dependent variables. The related table including the constant term and showing coefficients as changes in the z-scores is given in Appendix A3. Also, the results of a multinomial Probit specification are presented in Appendix A4 as a robustness check. Finally, the Wald chi-squares for all of these specifications are statistically significant (p <0.01), reflecting a high goodness of fit relative to the null specification.

VARIABLES	Upward trajectory			Downward trajectory		
	Upward Trajectory (U1 & U2)	Skimming (U1)	Quasi-Skimming (U2)	Market-Pricing (D1)	Quasi-Penetration (D2)	Penetration (D3)
Pricing strategy of predecessor [a]						
U1: Skimming	-0.122*	-0.050	-0.063	-0.123	0.055	0.256***
	[0.069]	[0.069]	[0.053]	[0.083]	[0.066]	[0.077]
U2: Quasi-skimming	-0.165***	-0.131**	-0.044	-0.041	0.087	0.208***
	[0.060]	[0.062]	[0.044]	[0.075]	[0.062]	[0.072]
D2: Quasi-penetration	-0.344***	-0.195***	-0.164***	0.058	0.115*	0.228***
	[0.070]	[0.068]	[0.057]	[0.077]	[0.060]	[0.074]
D3: Penetration	-0.260***	-0.173**	-0.093*	0.045	0.046	0.213***
	[0.070]	[0.069]	[0.049]	[0.078]	[0.057]	[0.077]
Feature core-ness [b]						
Weighted degree centrality	0.516*	0.478	0.044	0.084	0.173	-0.824***
	[0.303]	[0.300]	[0.206]	[0.309]	[0.148]	[0.266]
Betweenness centrality	-0.065	-0.132	-0.070	0.177	-0.440***	0.139
	[0.272]	[0.268]	[0.190]	[0.320]	[0.160]	[0.287]
Feature breadth						
Number of features	-0.025	0.021	-0.038*	-0.015	-0.010	0.033
	[0.027]	[0.025]	[0.021]	[0.030]	[0.017]	[0.024]
Number of feature clusters	-0.099**	-0.111**	-0.004	0.118**	-0.036	0.050
	[0.046]	[0.044]	[0.034]	[0.050]	[0.028]	[0.041]
Controls						
Introduction period	-0.019***	-0.013***	-0.008***	0.013***	-0.003	0.012***
	[0.003]	[0.003]	[0.003]	[0.004]	[0.002]	[0.004]
Post market takeoff	0.104	0.098	0.034	0.001	-0.066	-0.011
	[0.076]	[0.079]	[0.059]	[0.093]	[0.047]	[0.091]
Introductory product price	0.000***	0.000*	0.000***	-0.000	0.000	-0.001***
	[0.000]	[0.000]	[0.000]	[0.000]	[0.000]	[0.000]
Wald χ^2	101.41***	45.97***	62.18***	77.22***	42.82***	67.86***
Observations	367	367	367	367	367	367

Notes:
Coefficients show marginal effects of Probit regressions with robust standard errors in brackets
[a] Pricing strategy "D1: Market pricing" of predecessor as baseline
[b] An increase in feature core-ness amounts to a decrease in peripheral features
*** $p<0.01$, ** $p<0.05$, * $p<0.1$

Table 3: Probit Regressions of Pricing Strategies and Correlates

Interestingly, the predictive accuracy of our Probit models appears to be higher than what random heuristics would achieve. Consider the following two examples of such random heuristics based on our dataset: (1) about 42% of all products with a known predecessor will have an upward trajectory, and (2) the pricing strategy of a new product will match that of its predecessor in about 21% of the observed products. The Probit models shown in Table 3 and the multinomial model shown in Appendix A4 yield predictive accuracies that are about 2-3 times higher than such random heuristics would have. The fact that our models outperform such probabilistic benchmarks serves to validate the model specification.

The results support our hypotheses regarding the effect of strategic momentum. The use of a pricing strategy with a downward trajectory for a predecessor is positively correlated with the use of the same type of strategy (H1a), and negatively correlated with upward pricing trajectories (H1b), for the new product. The results thus imply that momentum continual is likely to occur when the predecessor follows a downward pricing strategy. Meanwhile, the use of a pricing strategy with an upward trajectory for a predecessor is positively correlated with the use of a downward pricing strategy (H2a), and negatively correlated with the use of the same type of strategy (H2b), for the new product. The effect of strategic momentum can also be seen from an analysis of proportions. Suppose we have an arbitrary pair of camera models (a_1, a_2), where a_1 is the predecessor and a_2 is the new model. Based on Figure 1, each camera model can follow one of five pricing strategies. Thus, the expected probability of both a_1 and a_2 having the exact same strategy (i.e., momentum continual) is $\frac{1}{5} \times \frac{1}{5} = \frac{1}{25} = 0.040$. A one-sample test of proportion suggests that the actual rate of an exact strategy match in our dataset (0.212) is significantly higher than the random expectation ($p < 0.01$). The expected probability of a_1 and a_2 having a strategy with the same trajectory (i.e., both strategies coming from either U1/U2 or D1/D2/D3) is $\frac{2}{5} \times \frac{2}{5} + \frac{3}{5} \times \frac{3}{5} = \frac{13}{25} = 0.520$. The actual rate of a trajectory-level match in the data is 0.528, which is quite high but not significantly different from the expected value ($p > 0.1$).

By contrast, the effects of feature composition are more surprising. According to hypothesis H3, an increase in peripheral features and feature breadth should be positively correlated with upward pricing trajectories (U1/U2) for new camera models. Based on hypothesis H4, we would expect a decrease in peripherals and feature breadth to correlate positively with downward pricing trajectories (D1/D2/D3). However, Table 3 appears to suggest the exact opposite of H3 and H4. A one-unit decrease in peripheral features increases the probability of an upward pricing trajectory by 51.6%. By contrast, a one-unit increase in peripherals is associated with a 44% and 82.4% increase in the chances of seeing the quasi-penetration (D2) and penetration (D3) strategies, respectively. As for feature breadth, a one-unit increase in the number of feature clusters correlates with a 9.9% decrease in the probability of an upward pricing trajectory, and an 11.1% decrease in seeing the skimming strategy (U1). Increasing the number of features by one unit also decreases the chance of seeing the quasi-skimming strategy (U2) by 3.8%. Finally, a one-unit increase in the number of feature clusters is associated with an 11.8% increase in the change of seeing the downward-oriented market pricing strategy (D1).

In the following, we propose a plausible explanation for the observed relationships between the pricing strategy and feature composition of a new product. First consider the inverse of H3, i.e., that an upward pricing trajectory should actually be positively correlated with a reduction in peripheral features and feature breadth. A firm may be able to justify an upward pricing trajectory (and potentially even an above-market introductory product price) if the feature reduction is framed as an effort to streamline the product design and reduce product complexity. Most consumers lack knowledge about novel features (especially if they are non-core), and thus make inferences about these based on limited information from past experience and the given context (Mukherjee & Hoyer, 2001; Rajendran & Tellis, 1994). Crucially, the empirical findings of Mukherjee and Hoyer (2001) suggest that, for high-complexity products such as cameras, more peripherals and feature breadth may cause a consumer to infer higher learning costs (e.g., inferring that more/new features will make a complex product more difficult to use and comprehend). Furthermore, purchasing a new product is an instance of a broader behavioral problem of decision-making under uncertainty. Most customers will typically not be early adopters and may therefore be averse to product complexity in such a purchase context (Moffatt et al., 2015; Sonsino et al., 2002).

Next, consider the inverse of H4, i.e., that a downward pricing trajectory should be positively correlated with an increase in peripheral features and feature breadth. Following from the above discussion, a consumer may not be able to fully appreciate the extent to which more features (especially peripherals) might add value to the base product (Thompson, Hamilton, & Rust, 2005). At the same time, however, the retailer may want to test new features and diffuse these in the market with the hope of becoming a standard-setter and securing a higher market share. Knowing that consumers may be wary of high-priced "beta products", the firm may be motivated to use a downward pricing strategy to aid rapid market diffusion (Stremersch & Tellis, 2002). The underlying assumption is that, despite being potentially price-conscious and viewing new features as "bloatware" (McCune, 1998), the consumer base may nevertheless be willing to endure the teething issues of the new product at a below-market price; this follows from the implications of extant literature on bundling in NPD, considering products as bundles of features (Reinders, Frambach, & Schoormans, 2010; Sarin, Sego, & Chanvarasuth, 2003).

Ironically, combining penetration pricing with feature bundling may essentially turn mainstream customers into reluctant early adopters of new products.

5. Conclusion and Discussion

Firms can use a variety of pricing strategies to launch new products into the market (Dean, 1976; Golder & Tellis, 2004; Tellis, 1986). The extant normative literature on pricing typically distinguishes between skimming and penetration as two fundamentally opposing views on dynamic pricing in relation to NPD (Monroe, 2003; Nagle et al., 2011). Skimming is primarily concerned with capturing value from a heterogeneous consumer base, and allows firms to effectively discriminate along multiple points of the demand curve from the outset (Tellis, 1986). By contrast, penetration pricing is based on the rationale of facilitating the diffusion of new products; rather than focusing on the price-inelastic demand of the high-end consumers, penetration pricing aims to entice the rest of the consumer base – especially the price-conscious or otherwise hesitant consumers – to try out the product, and potentially increases the rate of innovation adoption (Golder & Tellis, 2004).

Spann et al. (2015) classify dynamic pricing strategies by constructing a matrix of nine possible pricing strategies based on two levers: a product's introductory price (above, below or at the market price), and the subsequent pricing trajectory (above, below, or following the market trend). In this paper, we build on the work of Spann et al. by looking beyond firm and market-level correlates of the pricing strategies to consider aspects of the new product itself. Specifically, we investigate the effects of strategic momentum (i.e., whether a new product follows the pricing strategy of its predecessor) and feature composition (i.e., feature core-ness and breadth). Taking the five pricing strategies found by Spann et al. (2015) as outcome variables, we augment the related camera dataset by deriving correlates representing the predecessor's strategy and the new product's feature composition. Our subsequent analysis of the augmented camera dataset yields four main results. First, a continual of strategic momentum is observed when the strategy of the predecessor product has a downward trajectory. Second, a reversal of momentum is associated with an upward pricing trajectory of the predecessor. Third, increases in peripheral features and feature breadth are correlated with a downward pricing trajectory for the new product. Finally, decreases in peripheral features and feature breadth are associated with an upward pricing trajectory for new products.

The above results lead to some interesting theoretical implications. In general, our findings suggest that the predecessor's pricing strategy, and measures of feature composition and feature breadth can be viable correlates and predictors of the new product's pricing strategy. On the one hand, the effects of strategic momentum can be explained based on a reference pricing argument in the context of a competitive market. Spann et al. (2015) find the Herfindahl index of the market sample in the dataset to be 0.12, which indicates a high level of competitive intensity. The demand, shaped by the aggregation of consumers' reference prices, and reinforced by other factors (e.g., learning curve effects on the production side) can drive the firm to set product prices on a downward trajectory in general (Bayus, 1992; Kalish, 1983). Moreover, the high level of competition, coupled with the high rate of technology obsolescence in the case of consumer electronics (Mohr et al., 2010), may indicate that firms that use an upward pricing trajectory for one product will likely not be able to sustain this for the next product in the series. As such, our observed effects of strategic momentum seem to support extant research.

On the other hand, the results pertaining to feature composition are more surprising. The fact that we can provide plausible explanations for these results, which nevertheless go against our initial expectations, implies a case of competing hypotheses. The one set of hypotheses (H3 and H4) is guided by the idea that "more is better", i.e., packing the new product with more innovations should justify an above-market pricing trajectory. The second set of hypotheses (the inverse of H3 and H4) which appears to be supported by the actual data, captures the intriguing notion that "less is more", i.e., that more streamlined products can command higher prices. If consumers associate product innovation with product complexity (i.e., bloatware), then this may make it difficult for a high-priced product to compete with lower-priced, simpler alternatives (Mukherjee & Hoyer, 2001). Thus, framing feature reduction as an effort to streamline product design and improve consumer experience may allow firms to raise the perceived reference price of their products. For example, this "less is more" approach is reflected in the products developed by firms like Apple (e.g., removal of extraneous buttons and ports, and hiding/removing features that may be perceived as clutter). Firms may still be interested in "testing the waters" by bringing new innovations to the market, with the aim gaining an advantageous strategic position in the future (e.g., becoming a standard-setter of a new technology). As such, it may indeed make sense for firms to launch innovative, feature-rich new products at below-market prices to achieve more effective market penetration (Stremersch & Tellis, 2002). Technology firms such as Google and Microsoft, for instance, are known to test new features in mass-market product releases and benefit from indirect effects (e.g., via the dependencies of the new features with complementary products in the wider ecosystem) (Gawer & Cusumano, 2014).

The methodology and findings of this paper also offer insights for practitioners involved in NPD. In augmenting the camera dataset, we proposed a method to aggregate multiple predecessor strategies into a single measure and use network analysis to derive measures of feature composition. The problem of coding an approximate many-to-one mapping between products of a given series can be seen as a special case of the more general problem domain of "fuzzy matching" (Cormen, Leiserson, Rivest, & Stein, 2009; Navarro, 2001). Our manual approach to construct variables for capturing strategic momentum highlights the possible merit of using automated fuzzy methods to analyze latent patterns in conventional, relational marketing databases; such automated methods would scale to larger datasets. Similarly, our approach of constructing a feature co-occurrence matrix to derive measures of feature core-ness and breadth underscores the value of approaching questions in NPD by taking a network perspective. Using network measures represents an elegant and natural way of operationalizing concepts related to feature composition, and can be applied to other domains, such as the analysis of consumer purchase patterns (Dhar, Geva, Oestreicher-Singer, & Sundararajan, 2014; Videla-Cavieres & Rios, 2014) and path data (Hui, Fader, & Bradlow, 2009). The approaches of fuzzy matching and network analysis are increasingly available in the form of modular software packages that can be integrated into the analytics infrastructure of a firm's NPD department (Bastian et al., 2009; Provost & Fawcett, 2013). At a strategic level, our empirical findings also caution managers against taking a prescriptive view of the development and pricing of new products. As the surprising yet plausible results concerning the effects of feature composition demonstrate, the association between a particular set of product design choices (e.g., specifying the split between core and peripheral features in a product) and the pricing strategy at product launch may differ based on market conditions. Ultimately, our paper gives managers a more nuanced understanding of the link between aspects of the product itself and the corresponding pricing strategies. The resulting insights can help firms to assess the behavior of competitors in the same market (e.g., by being able to predict the likelihood of a competitor setting a certain pricing strategy based on past information about pricing and product composition). Our work can generally also help market analysts and policy makers to better understand the nature of dynamic pricing strategies in technology markets.

The main limitations of this study are related to the nature of our data set. Foremost, our approach only allows us to draw conclusions about correlational rather than causal relationships between the outcome and correlates. Second, we rely on the five pricing strategies identified by Spann et al. (2015) and thus their conceptualization of market price as a market average for the specific feature bundles of a product. Third, the results are based on a single dataset of one product category in one albeit large market. Future work can move towards addressing the abovementioned limitations and help establish the external validity of our findings by considering field data in the context of other product categories, sectors and geographies. Crucially, the results of a more expansive analysis may enable us to uncover boundary conditions for our hypotheses – especially with regards to the potentially competing sets of hypotheses related to feature composition (Ma, Gill, & Jiang, 2015; Nowlis & Simonson, 1996). Based on the availability of suitable data, future work may also look more closely at the interplay between pricing and feature composition over the course of a product's lifecycle (Day, 1981; Golder & Tellis, 2004; Ulrich & Eppinger, 2015).

Appendix

A1. Formal Definitions of Network Measures

We describe the formalizations in terms of a network $G = (V, E)$ with $|V|$ nodes and $|E|$ edges. The network can equally be described by a weighted matrix W, such that the element W_{ij} represents the strength of the edge between nodes i and j (e.g., frequency of co-occurrences in the case of event data). Let the adjacency matrix A_{ij} denote a non-weighted version of W_{ij}, such that the element $A_{ij} = 1$ if nodes i and j are connected and 0 otherwise. Below are the typical definitions of network measures used in our paper (Newman, 2010; Opsahl, Agneessens, & Skvoretz, 2010; Wasserman & Faust, 1994):

- **Weighted Degree Centrality** $C_D{}^W$ of node i: $C_D{}^W(i) = \sum_j^{|V|} W_{ij}$
- **Betweenness Centrality** C_B of node i: $C_B(i) = \frac{g_{jk}(i)}{g_{jk}}$, where g_{jk} denotes the number of shortest paths between nodes j and k, and $g_{jk}(i)$ of these paths go via node i.
- **Modularity Class** c of node i: The modularity of a network partition is given by $Q = \frac{1}{2m}\sum_{i,j}\left[W_{ij} - \frac{k_i k_j}{2m}\right]\delta(c_i, c_j)$, where $k_i = \sum_j W_{ij}$, c_i is the modularity class (or network community/cluster) to which node i is assigned, $\delta(c_i, c_j) = 1$ if $c_i = c_j$ and 0 otherwise, and $m = \frac{1}{2}\sum_{ij} W_{ij}$. The number of detected modularity classes per product constitutes a network measure for feature breadth in this paper, since it reflects the number of sub-product feature communities.

A2. Descriptive Data for Dichotomized Camera Features

Feature (present y/n)	Description	Weighted Degree	Betweenness	Modularity Class
OPT_FIND	Optical range finder	5184	34.730	1
LCD_FIND	LCD-monitor for finder	4903	33.538	0
AF_COD	Auto-focus	4246	39.147	4
FLASH_CO	Built-in flash	5358	39.147	3
CCD_CHIP	Uses CCD chip	4935	39.147	2
MEMO_CAR	Memory card slot	5304	39.147	0
SSFDC	SM card	966	2.481	1
COMFLASH	Compact flash	1899	5.811	5
SD_CARD	SD card	1356	7.448	3
XD_CARD	XD card	179	1.228	0
PC_CARD	PC card	8	0.000	1
MULTIMED	Multimedia card	73	1.459	1
MEMOSTIC	Memory stick	351	6.174	4
FLOPPY	Floppy disk support	85	2.125	2
CD	CD disc support	51	1.079	4
MP3_CO	MP3 player	111	2.518	1
BLTOO_CO	Bluetooth	10	0.000	1
PIX_CO_0_500	Pixel resolution (dichotomized into buckets of 500 pixels)	436	0.831	1
PIX_CO_500_1500		948	6.895	1
PIX_CO_1500_2500		1919	11.103	0
PIX_CO_2500_3500		1493	11.826	3
PIX_CO_3500_4500		638	10.920	4
PIX_CO_4500_5500		295	10.087	4
OPT_FAC_X1	Optical zoom factor (dichotomized by factor)	2160	8.860	1
OPT_FAC_X2		402	2.200	0
OPT_FAC_X3		2650	11.222	4
OPT_FAC_X4		170	0.619	4
OPT_FAC_X5		64	1.301	4
OPT_FAC_X6		43	0.194	2
OPT_FAC_X7		33	0.040	5
OPT_FAC_X8		91	3.369	2
OPT_FAC_X9		116	2.385	0
DIG_FAC_X1	Digital zoom factor (dichotomized by factor)	1182	10.524	1
DIG_FAC_X2		2088	7.987	5
DIG_FAC_X3		1138	3.107	0
DIG_FAC_X4		992	4.541	3
DIG_FAC_X5		44	0.363	4
DIG_FAC_X6		168	1.420	4
DIG_FAC_X7		33	0.293	4
DIG_FAC_X8		42	0.173	4
DIG_FAC_X9		21	0.063	4
DIG_FAC_X10		10	0.000	2
DIG_FAC_X11		11	0.000	4

Notes: Mean weighted degree centrality = 1214.093; Mean betweenness centrality = 8.500; Number of unique modularity groups = 6; Number of binary features in total = 43

Table A2: Descriptive Data for Dichotomized Camera Features

A3. Probit Regression (coefficients show changes in z-scores)

VARIABLES	Upward trajectory			Downward trajectory		
	Upward Trajectory (U1 & U2)	Skimming (U1)	Quasi-Skimming (U2)	Market-Pricing (D1)	Quasi-Penetration (D2)	Penetration (D3)
Pricing strategy of predecessor [a]						
U1: Skimming	-0.466*	-0.197	-0.412	-0.384	0.460	1.094***
	[0.267]	[0.272]	[0.347]	[0.263]	[0.543]	[0.347]
U2: Quasi-skimming	-0.632***	-0.516**	-0.284	-0.127	0.729	0.889***
	[0.236]	[0.248]	[0.287]	[0.235]	[0.507]	[0.321]
D2: Quasi-penetration	-1.319***	-0.769***	-1.069***	0.180	0.964*	0.972***
	[0.289]	[0.271]	[0.373]	[0.241]	[0.497]	[0.332]
D3: Penetration	-0.998***	-0.683**	-0.606*	0.140	0.383	0.911***
	[0.280]	[0.276]	[0.314]	[0.243]	[0.471]	[0.339]
Feature core-ness [b]						
Weighted degree centrality	1.979*	1.886	0.287	0.263	1.446	-3.520***
	[1.171]	[1.192]	[1.345]	[0.965]	[1.231]	[1.158]
Betweenness centrality	-0.251	-0.521	-0.459	0.552	-3.671***	0.593
	[1.041]	[1.057]	[1.237]	[1.003]	[1.373]	[1.227]
Feature breadth in product						
Number of features	-0.095	0.082	-0.249*	-0.048	-0.086	0.141
	[0.103]	[0.100]	[0.138]	[0.095]	[0.142]	[0.105]
Number of feature clusters	-0.380**	-0.439**	-0.024	0.369**	-0.302	0.213
	[0.180]	[0.173]	[0.220]	[0.158]	[0.239]	[0.175]
Controls						
Introduction period	-0.072***	-0.052***	-0.050***	0.041***	-0.025	0.051***
	[0.013]	[0.013]	[0.017]	[0.012]	[0.016]	[0.016]
Post market takeoff (1 = yes)	0.401	0.389	0.221	0.004	-0.548	-0.047
	[0.294]	[0.312]	[0.383]	[0.289]	[0.393]	[0.389]
Introductory product price	0.001***	0.001*	0.001***	-0.000	0.000	-0.002***
	[0.000]	[0.000]	[0.000]	[0.000]	[0.000]	[0.001]
Constant	2.472**	0.721	2.175*	-3.362***	2.480*	-2.113*
	[1.016]	[1.052]	[1.241]	[1.029]	[1.432]	[1.241]
Wald X^2	101.41***	45.97***	62.18***	77.22***	42.82***	67.86***
Observations	367	367	367	367	367	367

Notes:

Probit regressions with robust standard errors in brackets

[a] Pricing strategy "D1: Market pricing" of predecessor as baseline

[b] An increase in feature core-ness amounts to a decrease in peripheral features

*** $p<0.01$, ** $p<0.05$, * $p<0.1$

Table A3: Raw Probit Regressions (z-Scores) of Pricing Strategies and Correlates

A4. Multinomial Probit Regression (coefficients show marginal effects)

| | Upward trajectory | | Downward trajectory | | |
VARIABLES	Skimming (U1)	Quasi-Skimming (U2)	Market-Pricing (D1)	Quasi-Penetration (D2)	Penetration (D3)
Pricing strategy of predecessor [a]					
U1: Skimming	-0.071	-0.069	-0.161**	0.058	0.243***
	[0.066]	[0.053]	[0.082]	[0.062]	[0.078]
U2: Quasi-skimming	-0.145**	-0.049	-0.080	0.090	0.185**
	[0.061]	[0.044]	[0.074]	[0.058]	[0.072]
D2: Quasi-penetration	-0.203***	-0.163***	0.018	0.125**	0.224***
	[0.067]	[0.056]	[0.077]	[0.058]	[0.072]
D3: Penetration	-0.186***	-0.096*	0.016	0.052	0.214***
	[0.069]	[0.050]	[0.078]	[0.054]	[0.077]
Feature core-ness [b]					
Weighted degree centrality	0.512*	0.032	0.136	0.185	-0.864***
	[0.301]	[0.213]	[0.299]	[0.147]	[0.271]
Betweenness centrality	-0.021	-0.008	0.212	-0.404**	0.221
	[0.261]	[0.194]	[0.315]	[0.160]	[0.287]
Feature breadth					
Number of features	0.026	-0.037*	-0.010	-0.011	0.032
	[0.024]	[0.021]	[0.029]	[0.017]	[0.024]
Number of feature clusters	-0.115***	0.001	0.097**	-0.034	0.051
	[0.043]	[0.035]	[0.048]	[0.027]	[0.041]
Controls					
Introduction period	-0.013***	-0.007***	0.012***	-0.003	0.011***
	[0.003]	[0.003]	[0.004]	[0.002]	[0.004]
Post market takeoff	0.089	0.034	-0.028	-0.057	-0.038
	[0.074]	[0.056]	[0.089]	[0.046]	[0.088]
Introductory product price	0.000***	0.000***	0.000	0.000	-0.001***
	[0.000]	[0.000]	[0.000]	[0.000]	[0.000]
Observations	367	367	367	367	367

Notes:
Coefficients show marginal effects of a multinomial Probit regression with robust standard errors in brackets
The multinomial regression has a Wald X^2 statistic of 216.00 (p < 0.01)
[a] Pricing strategy "D1: Market pricing" of predecessor as baseline
[b] An increase in feature core-ness amounts to a decrease in peripheral features
*** p<0.01, ** p<0.05, * p<0.1

Table A4: Multinomial Probit Regressions of Pricing Strategies and Correlates

References

Abernathy, W. J., & Utterback, J. M. (1978). Patterns of industrial innovation. *Technology Review, 80*(7), 40–47.

Adler, P. S., & Clark, K. B. (1991). Behind the learning curve: A sketch of the learning process. *Management Science, 37*(3), 267–281.

Anderson, P., & Tushman, M. L. (1990). Technological discontinuities and dominant designs: A cyclical model of technological change. *Administrative Science Quarterly, 35*(4), 604–633.

Bastian, M., Heymann, S., & Jacomy, M. (2009). Gephi: an open source software for exploring and manipulating networks. *ICWSM, 8,* 361–362.

Bayus, B. L. (1992). The dynamic pricing of next generation consumer durables. *Marketing Science, 11*(3), 251–265.

Bertini, M., Ofek, E., & Ariely, D. (2009). The impact of add-on features on consumer product evaluations. *Journal of Consumer Research, 36*(1), 17–28.

Blondel, V. D., Guillaume, J.-L., Lambiotte, R., & Lefebvre, E. (2008). Fast unfolding of communities in large networks. *Journal of statistical mechanics: theory and experiment, 2008*(10), P10008.

Bolton, L. E., Warlop, L., & Alba, J. W. (2003). Consumer perceptions of price (un) fairness. *Journal of Consumer Research, 29*(4), 474–491.

Bowman, D., & Gatignon, H. (1996). Order of entry as a moderator of the effect of the marketing mix on market share. *Marketing Science, 15*(3), 222–242.

Carpenter, G. S., & Nakamoto, K. (1989). Consumer preference formation and pioneering advantage. *Journal of Marketing Research, 26*(3), 285–298.

Chaudhuri, H. R., & Majumdar, S. (2006). Of diamonds and desires: understanding conspicuous consumption from a contemporary marketing perspective. *Academy of Marketing Science Review, 2006,* 1.

Christensen, C. M., Suárez, F. F., & Utterback, J. M. (1998). Strategies for survival in fast-changing industries. *Management Science, 44*(12-part-2), S207-S220.

Cooper, M. J., Gutierrez, R. C., & Hameed, A. (2004). Market states and momentum. *The Journal of Finance, 59*(3), 1345–1365.

Cormen, T., Leiserson, C., Rivest, R., & Stein, C. (2009). *Introduction to algorithms* (3rd ed.): MIT Press.

Day, G. S. (1981). The product life cycle: analysis and applications issues. *The Journal of Marketing, 45*(4), 60–67.

Dean, J. (1976). Pricing policies for new products. *Harvard Business Review, 54*(6), 141–153.

Dhar, V., Geva, T., Oestreicher-Singer, G., & Sundararajan, A. (2014). Prediction in economic networks. *Information Systems Research, 25*(2), 264–284.

Ellison, G. (2005). A model of add-on pricing. *The Quarterly Journal of Economics, 120*(2), 585–637.

Gabaix, X., & Laibson, D. (2006). Shrouded attributes, consumer myopia, and information suppression in competitive markets. *The Quarterly Journal of Economics, 121*(2), 505–540.

Gatignon, H., Tushman, M. L., Smith, W., & Anderson, P. (2002). A structural approach to assessing innovation: Construct development of innovation locus, type, and characteristics. *Management Science, 48*(9), 1103–1122.

Gawer, A., & Cusumano, M. A. (2014). Industry platforms and ecosystem innovation. *Journal of Product Innovation Management, 31*(3), 417–433.

Gill, T. (2008). Convergent products: what functionalities add more value to the base? *Journal of Marketing, 72*(2), 46–62.

Golder, P. N., & Tellis, G. J. (1997). Will it ever fly? Modeling the takeoff of really new consumer durables. *Marketing Science, 16*(3), 256–270.

Golder, P. N., & Tellis, G. J. (2004). Growing, growing, gone: Cascades, diffusion, and turning points in the product life cycle. *Marketing Science, 23*(2), 207–218.

Guiltinan, J. P. (1987). The price bundling of services: A normative framework. *The Journal of Marketing, 51*(2), 74–85.

Hui, S. K., Fader, P. S., & Bradlow, E. T. (2009). Path data in marketing: An integrative framework and prospectus for model building. *Marketing Science, 28*(2), 320–335.

Kalish, S. (1983). Monopolist pricing with dynamic demand and production cost. *Marketing Science, 2*(2), 135–159.

Kalyanaram, G., & Winer, R. S. (1995). Empirical generalizations from reference price research. *Marketing Science, 14*(3), G161-G169.

Kotler, P., & Armstrong, G. M. (2014). *Principles of marketing* (15th ed.). Boston: Pearson.

Krishnan, V., & Ulrich, K. T. (2001). Product development decisions: A review of the literature. *Management Science, 47*(1), 1–21.

Liu, H. (2010). Dynamics of pricing in the video game console market: skimming or penetration? *Journal of Marketing Research, 47*(3), 428–443.

Ma, Z., Gill, T., & Jiang, Y. (2015). Core versus peripheral innovations: The effect of innovation locus on consumer adoption of new products. *Journal of Marketing Research, 52*(3), 309–324.

Mazumdar, T., Raj, S. P., & Sinha, I. (2005). Reference price research: Review and propositions. *Journal of Marketing, 69*(4), 84–102.

McCune, J. C. (1998). Technology's standard bearers. *Management Review, 87*(9), 43.

Meyer, R. J., Zhao, S., & Han, J. K. (2008). Biases in valuation vs. usage of innovative product features. *Marketing Science, 27*(6), 1083–1096.

Moffatt, P. G., Sitzia, S., & Zizzo, D. J. (2015). Heterogeneity in preferences towards complexity. *Journal of Risk and Uncertainty, 51*(2), 147–170.

Mohr, J. J., Sengupta, S., & Slater, S. F. (2010). *Marketing of high-technology products and innovations* (3rd ed.). Upper Saddle River, N.J.: Pearson.

Monroe, K. B. (2003). *Pricing: Making profitable decisions.* New York: McGraw-Hill.

Moreau, C. P., Lehmann, D. R., & Markman, A. B. (2001). Entrenched knowledge structures and consumer response to new products. *Journal of Marketing Research, 38*(1), 14–29.

Mukherjee, A., & Hoyer, W. D. (2001). The effect of novel attributes on product evaluation. *Journal of Consumer Research, 28*(3), 462–472.

Murmann, J. P., & Frenken, K. (2006). Toward a systematic framework for research on dominant designs, technological innovations, and industrial change. *Research Policy, 35*(7), 925–952.

Nagle, T. T., Zale, J., & Hogan, J. E. (2011). *The strategy and tactics of pricing: A guide to growing more profitably* (5th ed.). Upper Saddle River, N.J.: Prentice Hall.

Navarro, G. (2001). A guided tour to approximate string matching. *ACM computing surveys (CSUR), 33*(1), 31–88.

Newman, M. (2010). *Networks: An introduction.* New York: Oxford University Press.

Newman, M. E. J. (2005). A measure of betweenness centrality based on random walks. *Social Networks, 27*(1), 39–54.

Noble, P. M., & Gruca, T. S. (1999). Industrial pricing: Theory and managerial practice. *Marketing Science, 18*(3), 435–454.

Nowlis, S. M., & Simonson, I. (1996). The effect of new product features on brand choice. *Journal of Marketing Research, 33*(1), 36–46.

Opsahl, T., Agneessens, F., & Skvoretz, J. (2010). Node centrality in weighted networks: Generalizing degree and shortest paths. *Social Networks, 32*(3), 245–251.

Porter, M. E. (1979). How competitive forces shape strategy. *Harvard Business Review, 57*(2), 137–145.

Provost, F., & Fawcett, T. (2013). *Data science for business.* Sebastopol, CA: O'Reilly.

Rajendran, K. N., & Tellis, G. J. (1994). Contextual and temporal components of reference price. *The Journal of Marketing, 58*(1), 22–34.

Reinders, M. J., Frambach, R. T., & Schoormans, J. P. L. (2010). Using product bundling to facilitate the adoption process of radical innovations. *Journal of Product Innovation Management, 27*(7), 1127–1140.

Sarin, S., Sego, T., & Chanvarasuth, N. (2003). Strategic use of bundling for reducing consumers' perceived risk associated with the purchase of new high-tech products. *Journal of Marketing Theory and Practice, 11*(3), 71–83.

Simonson, I., Carmon, Z., & O'Curry, S. (1994). Experimental evidence on the negative effect of product features and sales promotions on brand choice. *Marketing Science, 13*(1), 23–40.

Sonsino, D., Benzion, U., & Mador, G. (2002). The complexity effects on choice with uncertainty-Experimental evidence. *The Economic Journal, 112*(482), 936–965.

Spann, M., Fischer, M., & Tellis, G. J. (2015). Skimming or penetration? Strategic dynamic pricing for new products. *Marketing Science, 34*(2), 235–249.

Stremersch, S., & Tellis, G. J. (2002). Strategic bundling of products and prices: A new synthesis for marketing. *Journal of Marketing, 66*(1), 55–72.

Tellis, G. J. (1986). Beyond the many faces of price: an integration of pricing strategies. *The Journal of Marketing, 50*(4), 146–160.

Thaler, R. (1985). Mental accounting and consumer choice. *Marketing Science, 4*(3), 199–214.

Thompson, D. V., & Norton, M. I. (2011). The social utility of feature creep. *Journal of Marketing Research, 48*(3), 555–565.

Thompson, D. V., Hamilton, R. W., & Rust, R. T. (2005). Feature fatigue: When product capabilities become too much of a good thing. *Journal of Marketing Research, 42*(4), 431–442.

Tushman, M., & Murmann, J. (1998). Dominant designs, technology cycles, and organizational outcomes. *Research in Organizational Behavior, 20,* 231–266.

Tushman, M. L., & Anderson, P. (1986). Technological discontinuities and organizational environments. *Administrative Science Quarterly, 31*(3), 439–465.

Ulrich, K. T., & Eppinger, S. D. (2015). *Product design and development* (6th ed.). New York: McGraw-Hill Education.

Varian, H. R. (2014). Big data: New tricks for econometrics. *The Journal of Economic Perspectives, 28*(2), 3–27.

Videla-Cavieres, I. F., & Rios, S. A. (2014). Extending market basket analysis with graph mining techniques: A real case. *Expert Systems with Applications, 41*(4), 1928–1936.

Wasserman, S., & Faust, K. (1994). *Social Network Analysis: Methods and Applications* (Vol. 8): Cambridge University Press.

Wathieu, L., & Bertini, M. (2007). Price as a stimulus to think: The case for willful overpricing. *Marketing Science, 26*(1), 118–129.

Essay 4:

Analyzing Consumer Behavior with Non-Tracking Event Data

Chinmay Kakatkar and Martin Spann

Abstract

With the increasing digitization of the retail industry, there is a growing abundance of event data describing consumer behavior (e.g., online clickstreams and offline sensors tracking the movement of shoppers). However, a large portion of the event data being generated cannot track individual consumers exactly, providing a wealth of what we call "non-tracking" event data. As evidenced by the recent calls for research, scholars and practitioners are increasingly recognizing the need for methods for analyzing event data in retailing. In response to the relative paucity of marketing research on non-tracking event data in retailing, this paper makes three interrelated methodological contributions. First, we suggest a classification of existing research pertaining to event data in retailing, which reveals the challenges of analyzing non-tracking event data. Second, we propose a methodology that takes a network perspective of event data and builds on past research to tackle the said challenges. Third, we validate the methodology using representative non-tracking event data collected by deploying sensor-enabled shelves in a field experiment within a store. We find that our method of analyzing event data can help uncover interesting patterns of in-store consumer behavior and could be applied across other retail settings in practice.

Keywords: Event Data, Network Analysis, Retail Marketing, Sensors, Internet of Things

1. Introduction

The retail sector as we know it is going digital and a number of retailers have begun to look at ways of exploiting digital innovations to better understand consumer behavior. In particular, retailers increasingly have access to event-based data, which captures a consumer's actions as a stream of events over time (e.g., an online clickstream or offline movement in a store). This trend is especially evident in B2C segments such as consumer goods and fashion (Moon & Ngai, 2008). A recent industry survey by Gorshe, Rollman, and Beverly (2012) suggests that executives are becoming more aware of the potential of item-level digital tracking to analyze customer-product interactions within a store and inform stocking decisions. For example, the fashion retailer Zara has successfully deployed sensors within its stores to increase offline sales and inventory accuracy. Burberry is another retailer that is often cited as a forward-thinking adopter of in-store technologies to better serve its customers (Batten, 2012). A customer shopping at a sensor-enabled Burberry store can watch product videos on "smart" mirrors in the changing rooms while trying on related items, and simultaneously browse relevant offers on a smartphone.

A key problem in practice, however, is that the event-based data collected by retailers cannot always be mapped one-to-one to the individual consumers that trigger the data. Yet, methods in extant literature have typically rested on the assumption that individuals can be tracked with a high degree of accuracy within event data. This assumption may be trivially valid for event data produced in a lab setting, as is the case with certain eye-tracking studies (Pieters & Warlop, 1999; Russo & Leclerc, 1994; Shi, Wedel, & Pieters, 2013). In the field setting, sensors generating the event data may need to move with the consumers to identify them uniquely; past studies have achieved this by attaching sensors to shopping baskets to track shopper movement patterns in physical stores (Hui, Bradlow, & Fader, 2009; Hui, Inman, Huang, & Suher, 2013). In contrast to the above situations, a sensor-enabled "smart shelf" is static – it can potentially detect the approach of consumers and their subsequent interactions with the displayed products, but may not be able to tell one individual apart from another (Inman & Nikolova, 2017).

Retailers could choose to deploy such "non-tracking" sensors for a number of reasons, despite the inability of the resulting event data to exactly identify individual consumers. For instance, the collection of non-tracking data may be attractive in terms of criteria such as cost-effectiveness, scalability, and privacy concerns from consumers in the age of "big data" (Bradlow, Gangwar, Kopalle, & Voleti, 2017). Developing methods to analyze non-tracking event data thus arguably represents a fruitful area for marketing research. Indeed, recent agenda-setting articles in top marketing journals have encouraged new research in this direction. Grewal, Roggeveen, and Nordfält (2016) have stressed the importance of understanding new technologies and data types in retail. Wedel and Kannan (2016) call for more work on diagnostic and predictive methods to support data-driven marketing decisions, especially in cases where the data may be sub-optimal in some respects (e.g., non-tracking event data).

In response to the relative paucity of marketing research on non-tracking event data in retail, this paper makes three interrelated methodological contributions. First, we suggest a classification of existing research pertaining to event data in retailing, and argue that the analysis of non-tracking data faces two key challenges: (1) the inability to identify individuals exactly, and (2) the difficulty of deriving contextually meaningful variables of interest from streams of event data. Second, we propose a methodology that takes a network perspective of event data and builds on past research to tackle the said challenges. Third, we collect representative non-tracking event data by deploying sensor-enabled shelves in a field experiment within a store to validate the methodology. We find that our method of analyzing event data can help uncover interesting patterns of in-store consumer behavior, and could be applied across other retail settings in practice.

2. Event Data in Retailing

A stream of events fundamentally captures a sequence of observable actions taken by one or more consumers in a given context over a period of time (Sismeiro & Bucklin, 2004). Table 1 presents one possible way of classifying event data in retailing, with the underlying aim of helping us to better position the value of our work in this paper. Specifically, we suggest that event data can be segmented based on the retail setting and the ability of the data to uniquely identify individual consumers. Note that the data structure of event streams is closely aligned with what Hui, Fader, and Bradlow (2009a) call "path data"; the authors provide a useful classification of path data, capturing situations as diverse as in-store shopping, online browsing and eye tracking. By contrast, our classification is more concerned with drawing attention to the challenges posed by non-tracking event data.

Non-tracking event data arguably poses two key challenges in online and offline retail settings. Firstly, by definition, non-tracking data does not afford the unique identification of individuals, which can either force researchers to analyze the data at an aggregate level, or endeavor to approximate individual identification in some way; our methodology takes the latter approach. Secondly, due to the relative simplicity of the data structure of events, deriving contextually meaningful variables of interest may not be straightforward. In contrast to survey scales or other variables captured in database marketing, raw event data (especially as collected by sensors in a retail store environment) typically does not expose variables that can be directly analyzed; this is more generally a problem of "big data", where the value of the data is derived not necessarily from the individual raw variables, but by combining them in contextually meaningful ways to facilitate deeper analysis (Bradlow et al., 2017; Wedel & Kannan, 2016). In the following, we summarize the nature of tracking and non-tracking event data across retail settings, commenting on related extant research – or the lack thereof – as appropriate. Note that this section of the paper should not be seen as an exhaustive literature review, but rather as a means to better position our subsequent methodology.

Retail Setting		Identification of Individual Consumers	
		Yes ("Tracking")	No ("Non-tracking")
Online		Click-streams when cookies are enabled; basic principle can be applied across devices (PC, mobile devices)	Anonymized click-streams, Media Metrix, data from Tor browser and Virtual Private Networks (VPNs)
Offline	Between-Store	Manual count data (e.g., from customer surveys), use of Beacons or similar technology, mobile targeting	Aggregate statistics of pedestrian foot traffic in malls, visitor counters at shop entrance
	In-Store	Bluetooth, attaching sensors/RFID tags to movable objects (shopping baskets, products), using eye-tracking technology	RFID-tagged or sensor-enabled smart shelves, walls and mirrors

Table 1: Classification of Event Data in Retail Marketing

2.1 Online

In the online setting, a retailer is ultimately part of a larger network of interconnected websites, which somewhat naturally leads to the analysis of user clickstreams as a way of analyzing user behavior (Bucklin & Sismeiro, 2009). Crucially, an individual's online activity may be tracked using "cookies", which can store and update pertinent information about a given website user over time – e.g., the IP address, location, language setting, browsing history (Miyazaki, 2008). Notwithstanding the privacy concerns surrounding their use, cookies and other seemingly more innocuous means of tracking – such as requesting a login before granting access to a website – allow researchers to uniquely map online activity to individuals. For example, Sherman and Deighton (2001) use cookies to measure the effectiveness of online banner ads and optimize their placement across different types of websites. Drèze and Hussherr (2003) are also concerned with improving banner effectiveness, but take a two-pronged approach of carrying out an eye-tracking lab study and a separate online survey. By mapping the eye movement patterns to individual subjects in the lab study, the authors find that previous research may have at times grossly overestimated the effectiveness of ads due to assuming that online users actually see the ads in the first place.

While the above studies make use of event data, their treatment of this data tends to simplify aspects of its essential nature (e.g., the type of events and their sequential dependencies). For instance, Sherman and Deighton (2001) are mainly interested in segmenting websites based on frequency of visits, which does not rely on knowing the paths that individual users take to reach any given website; the analyses may therefore implicitly be premised on the existence of discrete segments – rather than a continuum – of shopper behavior (Sorensen et al., 2017). Meanwhile, Drèze and Hussherr (2003) segment the eye-tracking event stream based on the location of fixations on the webpage; all fixation points in a particular part of the page are mapped to the same event. While this simplification or post-processing of the event stream has the benefit of making the subsequent analysis more tractable, it is not necessarily contextually meaningful; as the authors found, some of the more peripheral parts of the webpage were rarely visited by the subjects' eyes, but were nevertheless coded at a detailed level for the sake of completeness. However, online clickstream research has increasingly begun to leverage the inherent properties of the underlying event data more explicitly (Bucklin & Sismeiro, 2009; Hui et al., 2009a). Montgomery, Li, Srinivasan, and Liechty (2004) model the online purchase behavior of consumers by accounting for the actual sequence of events (website visits) that represent their browsing pattern. Sismeiro and Bucklin (2004) also model purchase behavior, but do so by segmenting the event data into contextually meaningful "task" variables. Crucially, in the absence of individual tracking, such methods become less feasible.

Non-tracking event data may arise in the online environment in at least two ways, namely due to data aggregation, and the anonymization of user details. Data may be aggregated at some higher level (e.g., user segment, geographical location, etc.) depending on the specific requirements of the researcher (Tellis, 2004). Data providers such as Media Metrix have been used by researchers in the past to obtain aggregated online event data. For example, Ilfeld and Winer (2002) used a Media Metrix panel to obtain data on average page views registered by websites to capture abstract concepts like loyalty and attention. Ghose and Yang (2009) comment on the widespread use of aggregated data and highlight its limited usefulness for the development of granular models of search engine advertising, although the authors stop short of suggesting a "workaround" that allows the use of such non-tracking data. Moreover, technological advances have allowed users to traverse the Internet more anonymously by using services such as Tor and Virtual Private Networks (Savchenko & Gatsenko, 2015). The key challenges posed by non-tracking data thus continue to remain relevant in the contemporary online setting. As we will show in Section 3, however, it may still be possible to build upon key elements of previous work on online clickstreams to develop methods for analyzing non-tracking event data.

2.2 Offline

Event data in an offline retail setting can broadly be constructed from the sequence of actions that a consumer takes in the physical environment (Hui et al., 2009a). Our decision to differentiate between-store and in-store event data in the classification in Table 1 mainly stems from the difference in the granularity of the respective data types, which in turn determines the kinds of analyses that can be done. Between-store event data may typically arise from the movement of consumers to a store starting from their home or another store (as in the case of a shopping mall). As Hui et al. (2009a) explain, such movement can be represented as a network of stores as nodes, where an edge between two nodes reflects the movement of a consumer between the corresponding stores. The same principle can be applied to the in-store context as well. If between-store data is taken to represent a consumer's "macro-level" spatial movement, then in-store data can capture "micro-level" movement (e.g., between aisles rather than stores).

The work by Mazze (1974) provides an early example of between-store data that tracks individuals, albeit without any advanced sensor-based technology. The author conducts a study in which subjects are asked to manually keep a log of their travels to stores; each raw event in this dataset corresponds to the location of a subject at a given point in time. By superimposing the event sequences on a geographical map, Mazze was able to analyze the effect of the subjects' demographics (e.g., gender) on their travel distance, and the nature of patronage with regards to the purchase of convenience goods (e.g., not always going to the "usual" store). More recently, the spread of mobile technology has created a new avenue for tracking between-store data. In particular, it is possible to obtain information on a consumer's current location based on the data collected by their mobile devices (e.g., GPS and/or WIFI-enabled smartphones). The increasing abundance of such information has accelerated research on topics such as mobile targeting (Luo, Andrews, Fang, & Phang, 2013) and location-based advertising (Molitor, Reichhart, Spann, & Ghose, 2016). In both cases, the opportunity to derive marketing insights comes from leveraging the temporal and spatial sequences of a consumer's physical location; being in a certain locale at a given time or moving in the direction of a store may make a location-based marketing message – ranging from a passive information update to a more active call to action or promotional offer – seem more relevant to the consumer than another message that does not take the locational data into account.

Recent technological advances have also enabled the generation of event data that tracks consumers within stores (Burke, 2010). For example, the use of Bluetooth technology represents an instance of the basic approach to consumer tracking already used in the between-store context discussed above (Sorensen et al., 2017). Whereas GPS and IP-based location tracking is more appropriate for macro-level data collection, matching Bluetooth signals to consumers' mobile devices can facilitate micro-level, in-store tracking. Phua, Page, and Bogomolova (2015) track the event data emitted by Bluetooth-enabled devices to investigate the length of shopping trips and the representativeness of the Bluetooth sample within a supermarket; additional demographic data obtained by surveying the shoppers in the same store is then matched with the event data to derive further covariates for later statistical analyses. In-store event data that tracks individuals can also be generated by attaching sensors or RFID-tags to shopping carts/baskets which move with the consumer through the store. The PathTracker® system is an example of such shopping cart tracking, and has been used in a number of previous studies to analyze and model in-store movement patterns of shoppers (Hui, Bradlow et al., 2009; Hui et al., 2013; Larson, Bradlow, & Fader, 2005; Sorensen et al., 2017).

Crucially, the above examples of research based on offline event data rely on the ability to match the events to unique individuals, and make sense of the events by leveraging contextually meaningful variables (Bradlow et al., 2017; Hui et al., 2009a) – yet both of these aspects constitute key challenges in the case of non-tracking event data. Past research has often taken the approach of aggregating non-tracking event data (Ghose & Yang, 2009; Tellis, 2004). For instance, extant literature has demonstrated the possibility of aggregating between-store and in-store pedestrian traffic to infer the popularity of stores, products and promotional campaigns (Granbois, 1968; Underhill, 2000). Note that, depending on the research question, aggregating event data may be a perfectly appropriate approach; it ultimately allows researchers to analyze the difference in statistics (e.g., mean, standard deviation) between the groups (i.e., at the level of data aggregation).

However, such data is not ideal for answering questions that relate to the sequential nature of the events. Increasingly, retailers are deploying "smart" technology – embedded in shelves, mirrors and walls – that cannot follow consumers like a shopping cart would, leading to an abundance of non-tracking event data (Inman & Nikolova, 2017). Note that while initial evidence suggests that the untapped potential of non-tracking event data may be especially significant for in-store use-cases, the general arguments favoring non-tracking data over the tracking alternative (e.g., cost, scalability and privacy) are applicable to between-store and online scenarios also (Aguirre, Mahr, Grewal, Ruyter, & Wetzels, 2015; Bradlow et al., 2017; Bughin, Chui, & Manyika, 2015). In this context, scholars across research domains in retail have issued calls for further research that encompasses the development of "practice-driving" methodologies to analyze non-tracking event data (Grewal et al., 2016; Rafaeli et al., 2017; Wedel & Kannan, 2016). In the next section, we outline our methodology to analyze non-tracking event data on an individual level.

3. Methodology

Hui et al. (2009a) present a useful integrative framework for thinking about the paths of agents (i.e., their sequences of movement) in online and offline environments, and we use this as a starting point to conceptualize our view of event data. Based on Hui et al., an agent's path can be defined as a tuple $P = \{L, A, X_A(t)\}$, where L denotes the location or environment (e.g., online, between-store or in-store), A denotes the conscious agent, and $X_A(t)$ captures the agent's position at time t in the given spatial environment. We can intuitively see how a path P might be constructed in the examples of event data discussed in Section 2. For example, in the between-store research by Mazze (1974), L would be the geographical location of each study subject A, and X_A would give the movement pattern of the subjects over time. In the studies using the PathTracker® system (Hui et al., 2013; Larson et al., 2005), L can be a store or mall, A the shopper, and X_A her physical movement pattern. Interestingly, the environment in a between-store setting may be essentially discrete (the subject can move from store to store), while in the in-store setting it is more continuous (the shopper can move anywhere on the shop floor). As Hui et al. (2009a) note, a discrete environment can be represented as a network of nodes that define an agent's movement space.

Based on the above intuition, we formalize event data as follows. Let E denote a finite set of events $\{e_1, e_2, \dots\}$. These events may be emitted by a physical sensor embedded in a smart shelf that tracks passing consumers in a store (Guralnik & Srivastava, 1999; Inman & Nikolova, 2017), or an online analytics system that tracks the clickstreams of web users (Bucklin & Sismeiro, 2009). An important consequence of the finiteness of E is that the range of observable events a consumer can trigger is inherently restricted by the size of E. Next, let S denote a finite set of "artifacts" $\{s_1, s_2, \dots\}$. Artifacts can be thought of as those entities in the environment that are able to emit events in response to the consumer's behavior. Sensor-enabled shelves in a store, or shop doors mounted with visitor counters, are examples of artifacts. In contrast to the abstract nature of the framework presented by Hui et al. (2009a), our methodology is more managerially oriented, such that we find it useful to explicitly specify artifacts as entities of interest in the consumer's environment. Finally, we let a finite set $A = \{a_1, a_2, \dots\}$ denote the agents (or consumers). Then a stream of event data, say Q, is given by a vector of time-indexed events, e.g., $[e_1, e_2, e_1, e_2, e_3, \dots]$, which is produced by the interaction of consumers with artifacts in their environment. Note that, although Hui et al. (2009a) formalize the path P of a particular agent, we can at best approximate such a path in non-tracking event data. Event streams can broadly be thought of as point processes (Cox & Isham, 1980), as seen in past marketing research using online path data (Li & Kannan, 2014; Xu, Duan, & Whinston, 2014). Notice also that the sequence of events can be in any order as long as this is permitted by the real-world constraints on the consumer's behavior. For example, transitioning from an event e_1 (say, entering a store) to an event e_3 (picking up a product) may necessarily trigger an event e_2 (arriving at the product display) in between.

In the following sections, we build on the above concepts to present a methodology for analyzing non-tracking event data with three related design goals in mind. First, the method should address the two challenges of analyzing non-tracking event data, namely identifying individuals (at least approximately) and deriving contextually relevant variables. Second, it should in principle be possible to apply the method to scenarios involving non-tracking event data across the online and offline settings classified in Table 1; this implies that the method should be modular, i.e., one component can be swapped for an alternative without significantly affecting the rest of the method workflow. Third, it should be possible for a retailer to implement the method in practice, by building on top of existing technological infrastructure like sensor-enabled artifacts and web analytics software. Figure 1 provides a high-level, process-oriented overview of our proposed methodology. Note that, to help readers visualize the implementation details in a concrete retail setting, we mainly focus on an in-store context. Also, to simplify the exposition of our approach, we initially consider the simple case of a single consumer interacting with a single artifact at any given point in time. We then discuss how our method can be extended to allow analysis of consumer behavior in more complex cases (e.g., many consumers and many artifacts).

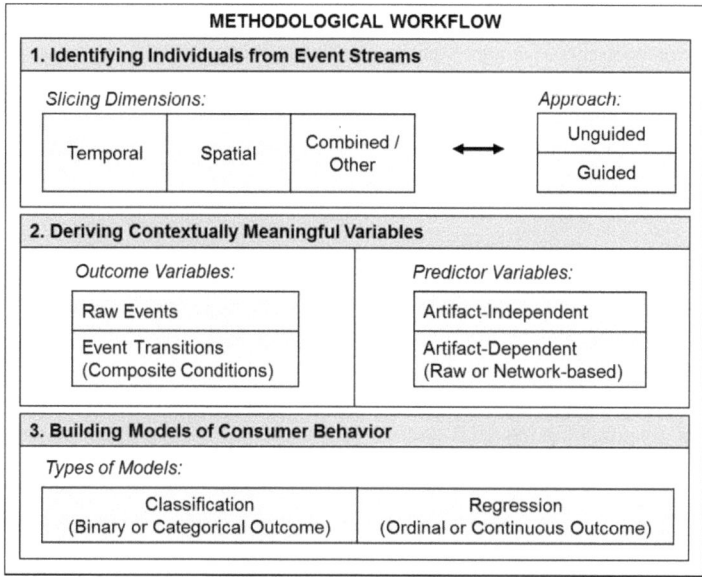

Figure 1: Overview of Methodological Workflow

3.1 Identifying Individuals from Event Streams

We begin by tackling the challenge of approximately identifying individuals with non-tracking event data. Consider an event stream capturing a consumer's interaction with a product on a sensor-enabled shelf in a store. Each observation in the non-tracking dataset will likely be timestamped, stating the type of event and the artifact where the event was triggered. In the simple case of a single consumer (regardless of how many artifacts there are) we can identify the individual at all times. However, as soon as we allow for multiple consumers, it is no longer obvious from the raw (non-tracking) event data, whether two adjacent events $[\dots, e_i, e_j, \dots]$ were triggered by the same consumer or by two different ones. Ideally, we would like to split up a given event sequence into several slices, each of which contain the events triggered by a unique individual; this way, although events that occur close to each other in the raw event stream might be more likely to correspond to the same individual, it is still possible for us to later map the events to different individuals.

3.1.1 Slicing Dimensions

Extant literature on information retrieval algorithms and data mining suggests that there are at least three heuristics for slicing the event stream: temporal, spatial and combined/other (Kumar, Mahadevan, & Sivakumar, 2004; Nagarajan et al., 2009; Yang, Pierce, & Carbonell, 1998). Using temporal slicing, we can assume events that occur in the same time interval belong to the same individual. The size of the time interval is clearly an important slicing parameter, since a slice that is too large or too small may produce an inaccurate mapping of events to individuals. In spatial slicing, events that occur at artifacts that are located close together are grouped into a slice. The extent to which spatial slicing on its own is meaningful depends on the specific context. For example, spatial slicing may be useful in situations where there are several artifacts that are spaced far apart, as in a between-store context (Mazze, 1974; Pennacchioli, Coscia, Rinzivillo, Pedreschi, & Giannotti, 2013). Finally, the slicing heuristic might combine temporal and spatial elements, and leverage additional situational data; this may involve augmenting the event data with information from related datasets.

Given the alternatives, we use temporal slicing in this paper for three practical reasons. First, temporal slicing can leverage the fact that event streams are typically ordered by time to begin with, so sorting the data again is not required. By casting the timestamps to numerical data types, one can slice the event stream using division and modulo arithmetic operators in a fairly convenient manner (Cox, 2007). Temporal slicing is thus simple to implement from a practitioner's perspective. Second, slicing by time may offer more variation than slicing by spatial location, which could be a valuable property depending on the context. Unlike artifacts – whose number is essentially fixed (e.g., the set of shelves in a store) – we have more freedom in varying the size of temporal slices. For instance, the same one-hour block of time can be sliced by minute, second, or millisecond; our choice of the slice size may depend on considerations such as the rate at which events are typically emitted in the given context, and what that implies for the identification of individuals. Lastly, consumer behavior in a temporally sliced event stream can be analyzed using panel data methods, assuming that the set of artifacts largely remains unchanged over time; in particular, the time slicing yields the time variable and the artifact becomes the panel variable (Wooldridge, 2013, pp. 484–499). These empirical considerations are discussed in more detail in Section 3.3.

3.1.2 Unguided or Guided Slicing

Suppose the event stream $Q = [e_1, e_2, e_3, e_4, e_1, e_2, e_1, e_2, e_3, e_2, e_3, e_4]$ represents a consumer's activity in a store, such as approaching a smart shelf (e_1), picking up (e_2) and putting down (e_3) the displayed product, and then leaving the shelf (e_4). To now slice the data along the dimension of time, we can broadly opt for one of two approaches (Kimball & Ross, 2009), namely unguided and guided slicing. The unguided approach assumes that the consumer's activity is linear in time, i.e., that the time between adjacent events is always the same. Given a stream of n events, we would slice the stream into k pieces with $\lfloor n/k \rfloor$ events per slice. For example, if $k = 3$, then the above event stream would be sliced into $Q_U = [[e_1, e_2, e_3, e_4], [e_1, e_2, e_1, e_2], [e_3, e_2, e_3, e_4]]$. The upside of unguided slicing is that it is cheap to implement, easy to test the robustness of different choices of the slicing parameter k, and interpreting aggregate statistics (e.g., averages) at the level of slices is straightforward. However, the linearity assumption underlying the unguided approach may not always be satisfied by the actual frequency of the event occurrences over time. Thus, a major downside is that the unguided derivation of slices is essentially arbitrary and may not map well to the set of actual unobserved individuals.

By contrast, guided slicing does not make the linearity assumption, and seeks instead to leverage outside information based on the retailer's past experience or preliminary analyses (qualitative and quantitative) of consumers in the store setting. As such, guided slicing might split the above event stream into $Q_G = [[e_1, e_2, e_3, e_4], [e_1, e_2], [e_1, e_2, e_3, e_2, e_3, e_4]]$. Notice that the slices in Q_G may not necessarily be evenly sized, which makes the interpretation of slice-level aggregate statistics more difficult. For example, the event e_2 makes up 50% and 33% of the events respectively in the second and third slices of Q_G, but occurs more often in the third slice. However, in terms of addressing the challenge of identifying individuals in non-tracking event data, guided slicing is preferable where possible, since the guided set of slices can potentially approximate the actual individual set more closely than in the unguided approach. In practice, the trade-off between the unguided and guided approaches can arguably only be resolved on a case-by-case basis.

3.2 Deriving Contextually Meaningful Variables

Next we tackle the problem of deriving contextually meaningful outcome variables and corresponding predictors from non-tracking event data. Recall from the classification in Table 1 that event data can arise in various retail settings, and that the meanings of individual events and event transitions may differ accordingly. In practice, retailers would ideally like a tractable analytical procedure to discover variables that provide insights about consumer behavior. To this end, our methodology takes a network perspective on the problem of variable derivation. Examples of the two main types of networks are depicted in Figures 2(a) and 2(b).

The event network as represented in Figure 2(a) is often referred to as a "transition diagram" in engineering disciplines (Wang, 2013, pp. 4–5). The set of nodes in the event network consists of all unique events seen in the event stream; a directed edge between two nodes represents a permissible event transition. Thus, the network in Figure 2(a) might have been constructed from the event stream $[e_1, e_2, e_3, e_3, e_2, e_1]$, which is incidentally also the shortest such stream that could lead to the given event network. Moreover, event streams in a retail setting must start with an initial event (e.g., a consumer entering a store), and this corresponds to the entry point into the event network. In our example, the initial event happens to be e_1. An event transition matrix can now be computed, in which the element in the j-th row and the i-th column of the matrix captures the frequency (or proportion) of transitions from event e_i to event e_j in the event stream. The event network then emerges naturally from the transition matrix, such that nodes represent the event types and the edges denote event transitions. Note that, while clickstream research has previously used event transition matrices in Markovian analyses (Montgomery et al., 2004), we use such matrices to operationalize our network perspective and thus construct contextually meaningful outcome variables as discussed in the next section.

Interestingly, whereas the event network emerges directly from the event stream, the artifact network is derived by "chaining together" the artifacts at which these events are triggered over time. In this sense, the event and artifact networks conceptually exist at two different levels. Notice that the existence of an artifact network with more than one node assumes a retail setting with more than one artifact, but makes no claim about the number of consumers. The example in Figure 2(b) depicts five nodes/artifacts (e.g., sensor-enabled shelves), and the edges imply adjacency in the event stream. The edges may correspond to the actions of a single consumer triggering events at each artifact sequentially, or many consumers triggering events at different artifacts simultaneously. Distinguishing between the cases of single and many consumers requires an understanding of the constraints imposed on the actions of individual consumers in the given retail context. For instance, it may be unlikely for events occurring in a very short timeframe at two ends of a store to be triggered by the same consumer.

Taking a network perspective on non-tracking event data offers at least two main benefits in terms of deriving contextually meaningful variables. First, the relational nature of event transitions and an individual's movement between artifacts lends itself naturally to a network-based conceptualization (Hui et al., 2009a). The network representations are both theoretically appealing and intuitive to implement in practice. Second, casting the event data as a web of relationships between events/artifacts creates opportunities for applying methods from network analysis to generate outcome variables and associated predictors (Newman, 2010; Wasserman & Faust, 1994). As we demonstrate in the following sections, the event network can be especially useful for deriving outcome variables, while the artifact network can yield interesting situational predictors.

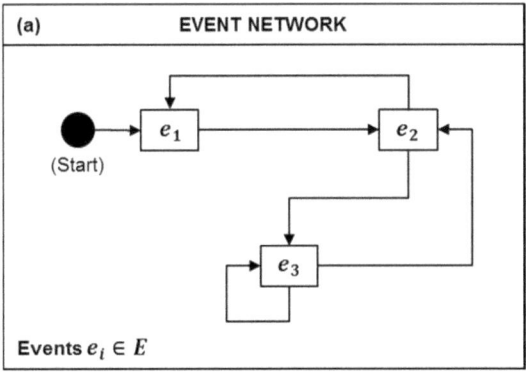

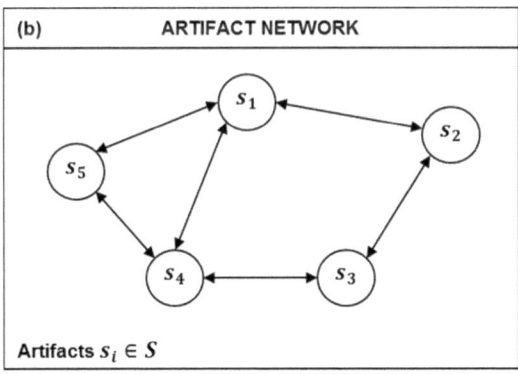

Figure 2: Examples of Multi-Level Network Views on Event Data

3.2.1 Outcome Variables

In the following, we discuss two types of outcome variables that can be derived from non-tracking event data – the raw events themselves, and conditions constructed from event transitions. Whether a raw event is meaningful in terms of its frequency of occurrence, duration or other properties depends on various aspects of the data collection setup. For instance, consider a hypothetical sensor that is calibrated to record an event when a consumer passing by a shelf picks up a product and places it in the shopping cart; this action may indeed be worth analyzing as an outcome variable in its own right (Hui, Fader, & Bradlow, 2009b; Larson et al., 2005). Despite being a single raw event, such a variable may be a useful proxy for a more abstract concept like purchase intent.

The above hypothetical event can also be broken down into smaller, atomic events such as "visit shelf", "pick up product" and so on. It is these atomic events that are typically captured as raw data by sensors deployed in typical retail settings – especially those affixed to stationary artifacts in offline environments (Guralnik & Srivastava, 1999). One approach to construct meaningful outcome variables from atomic events may be to consider the transitions between events in more detail. Building on the work by Montgomery et al. (2004), we can construct a matrix M that describes the conditional probability of each event transition in a given context. The element m_{ji} in M denotes $P(e_j|e_i)$, the probability of event e_j following e_i in the event stream. The conditional probability for each pair of adjacent events can be derived by taking a frequentist view of the event data. In general, an event stream of n raw events will yield $n-1$ adjacent event pairs.

For example, consider the event stream $Q = [e_1, e_2, e_3, e_4, e_1, e_2, e_1, e_2, e_3, e_2, e_3, e_4]$. Q consists of 12 raw events that can be grouped into the following 11 adjacent event pairs: (e_1, e_2), (e_2, e_3), (e_3, e_4), (e_4, e_1), (e_1, e_2), (e_2, e_1), (e_1, e_2), (e_2, e_3), (e_3, e_2), (e_2, e_3) and (e_3, e_4). Counting the number of occurrences of each observed transition (e_i, e_j) in Q yields the frequency matrix of j rows and i columns,

$$F = \begin{pmatrix} 0 & 1 & 0 & 1 \\ 3 & 0 & 1 & 0 \\ 0 & 3 & 0 & 0 \\ 0 & 0 & 2 & 0 \end{pmatrix},$$

and the corresponding transition probability matrix,

$$M = \begin{pmatrix} 0 & 1/2 & 0 & 1/2 \\ 3/4 & 0 & 1/4 & 0 \\ 0 & 1 & 0 & 0 \\ 0 & 0 & 1 & 0 \end{pmatrix}.$$

Notice in matrix M that, for example, $P(e_2|e_3) = 1/4$; that is, $P(e_j|e_i)$ is the probability of seeing e_j immediately after e_i in the event stream, rather than seeing event e_j in general. If the set E of permissible events is sufficiently small and the event stream registers at least one occurrence of each $e_j \in E$ following some other event, then it is intuitive to see that the frequency matrix F will not be too sparse, so that each row of M will sum to 1.

Crucially, we can now combine the probabilities in M to derive composite conditions that may represent contextually relevant outcome variables. The kind of composite conditions we consider in this paper are of the form $\sum_{j=1}^{k} \sum_{i=1}^{k} \omega_{ji} P(e_j|e_i) > \theta$, where the event set E consists of k unique events, $\omega_{ji} \in [-1,0,1]$ is a weighting that essentially serves the purpose of including/excluding certain probabilities $P(e_j|e_i)$ from the condition (although we could let $\omega_{ji} \in \mathbb{R}$ in general), and θ represents a threshold value above which the conditional is true. The above formulation is fairly parsimonious, while giving us significant flexibility in composing conditions of varying complexities. For example, $P(e_2|e_1) > 0$ is a simple condition which asserts that the transition from e_1 to e_2 occurs at least once in the event stream. The condition $P(e_2|e_1) - P(e_2|e_3) > 0$ is more complex, asserting that the transition from e_1 to e_2 has a higher probability of occurring than the transition from e_3 to e_2 in the event stream. We show in Section 4 how such composite conditions can be used to operationalize outcomes related to customer-product interactions inside a physical store in a contextually meaningful manner.

3.2.2 Predictors

Based on the formalization of event data described earlier, we differentiate between two types of predictors: artifact-independent and artifact-dependent. Predictors that exist independently of artifacts may include variables that are temporal (e.g., time of day, day of the week) or situational (e.g., the number and nature of salespeople in a store, promotional offers and loyalty programs). Clearly, any number of these variables may potentially be good predictors of a given outcome variable, and should thus be incorporated in the analysis where appropriate. However, the work by Bradlow et al. (2017) – along with our own experience of working with retailers –

suggests that artifact-independent "big data" is not the same as "better data". The notion of big data mainly concerns the objective dimension of the data, such as its volume, variety and velocity (Diebold, 2012), without necessarily making any claim about the usefulness of the data to the business. A retailer might collect vast amounts of data from multiple sources, but these may be stored in a fragmented manner that makes it difficult to match them to individual consumers.

Meanwhile, artifact-dependent predictors are those variables that are derived from the artifacts themselves. Such variables are fixed for a given artifact and may be time-invariant; they can thus be loosely thought of as artifact-specific effects (Wooldridge, 2013, pp. 484–485). For example, an in-store artifact may consist of variables such as the attributes of a smart shelf, the shelf's location on the shop floor, and the attributes of the product displayed on the shelf. Each of these variables can take on different values for each artifact, depending on the decisions made by the store manager (e.g., whether to change the displayed product or shelf location). Raw artifact-dependent variables may be incorporated into the analysis of consumer behavior in much the same way as the artifact-independent variables discussed previously; after all, both sets of variables offer raw, observable measures of the given retail context. We can also leverage the relational view of artifacts as shown in Figure 2(b) to derive meta-level network measures to serve as artifact-dependent predictors. For example, by applying network analysis to the artifact network, we can compute measures of an artifact's "influence" (e.g., degree centrality) and its place in the network's structure (e.g., which cluster of nodes it belongs to) (Newman, 2010). Note that, in contrast to a social network, an artifact network reflects the aggregate actions of agents/consumers outside the network (Borgatti, Mehra, Brass, & Labianca, 2009; Dhar, Geva, Oestreicher-Singer, & Sundararajan, 2014).

To see the subtle similarities and differences between raw and network-based measures related to artifacts, consider the sets $X = \{x_1, x_2\}$ and $Z = \{z_1, z_2\}$ of two raw variables x_1 and x_2 (e.g., location in store and type of displayed product), and two network-based measures z_1 and z_2 (e.g., degree and betweenness centrality) respectively. These variables would be mapped to a set S of artifacts. As such, let the function $v_s(\cdot)$ return the value of a measure for a given artifact s. Now suppose we have two artifacts, s_1 and s_2. Since X and Z are artifact-dependent predictors, we can by definition always obtain a set of values $\{v_s(x_1), v_s(x_2), v_s(z_1), v_s(z_2)\}$ (where $s = s_1, s_2$); this set of values represents the association between artifacts and their measures. However, for a small set X whose elements take on discrete values, it may be that the function $v_s(\cdot)$ returns the same value for both artifacts s_1 and s_2. The artifacts may both be at the same location (e.g., "near the entrance"), such that

$v_{s_1}(x_1) = v_{s_2}(x_1)$, or display the same product, such that $v_{s_1}(x_2) = v_{s_2}(x_2)$; this may be entirely plausible in a real retail context, as we show in the empirical study in Section 4. By contrast, if the artifact network is not fully connected (i.e., all nodes are not linked to all other nodes), then it will be rare to find $v_{s_1}(z) = v_{s_2}(z)$ for network measures $z \in Z$, since they tend to take on a greater variety of values; a single incoming or outgoing edge can cause a given network statistic to change between nodes. Crucially, the additional heterogeneity in the values of network measures is desirable for us, since it can potentially explain more of the variance in an outcome variable (Wooldridge, 2013, pp. 69–72), and hence improve predictive performance.

3.3 Building Models of Consumer Behavior

3.3.1 Consumer-Artifact Interactions as Panel Data

Suppose that our retail context consists of N artifacts, and we temporally slice the corresponding event stream into T time intervals, with each such interval representing an individual consumer. Then we have an $N \times T$ panel of artifacts observed over the set of all consumers that appear in the event data. Given an outcome variable of interest (e.g., whether a consumer interacts with a product), say y, we can construct the linear model $y_{it} = \alpha + \beta X_i + \gamma Z_i + \varphi C_{it} + \varepsilon$ for $i = 1, \dots, N$ and $t = 1, \dots, T$, where y_{it} is the outcome variable observed for consumer t at artifact i, α is the average effect, X and Z are vectors of artifact-dependent predictors (raw and network-based, respectively), C is the vector of artifact-independent predictors, and ε is the composite error term. Now, if the individual-specific predictors are uncorrelated with the artifact-dependent ones, then we can estimate the outcome variable using a random effects (RE) model (Wooldridge, 2013, pp. 492–493). The related specification test proposed by Hausman (1978) can be used to gauge the appropriateness of using the RE model as opposed to the somewhat stricter fixed effects (FE) model. Unlike the FE model, the RE model assumes that the unobserved heterogeneity is uncorrelated with the individual-specific predictors and thus includes it in the composite error term ε.

In general, by treating the consumer-artifact interactions as panel data and estimating the outcome using an effects model, we are able to control for unobserved heterogeneity. If the outcome variable is binary or categorical, we would treat it as count data using a suitable classification model (e.g., a Logit or Negative Binomial), whereas we would apply a regression model (e.g., ordered Probit or OLS) to an ordinal or continuous outcome variable. Other non-linear algorithms (e.g., decision trees and random forests) typically encountered in machine learning could also be applied (Varian, 2014). However, we would argue that the crucial insight here concerns the initial choice of heuristic (e.g., temporal or spatial) for slicing the non-tracking event data, and the conceptualization of artifacts, at the outset of our methodology. Viewed "backwards" from the perspective of panel data analysis, it is clear that the slicing heuristic should afford sufficient variation in the consumer-artifact interaction. For instance, opting for temporal instead of spatial slicing may produce more slices, thus yielding a richer panel dataset that could approximate the between-consumer heterogeneity more accurately. Similarly, by finding the right balance in the number and complexity of the contextual components used to define artifacts, the resulting panel data can enable a nuanced analysis that accounts for within-consumer variation.

3.3.2 Many Consumers and Many Artifacts

The two fundamental entities in our retail-oriented conceptualization of event data are the consumers and the artifacts that they interact with. The cases of a single consumer interacting with one or more artifacts over time are covered by our methodological exposition so far. By defining artifacts and slicing the event data to approximate individual consumers, we allow for consumers to interact with different artifacts, notwithstanding the constraints imposed by the event network (e.g., some event transitions may be impossible) and the organization of the artifacts (e.g., distal artifacts are harder to reach for a consumer).

What happens if we allow two or more consumers to interact with the same artifact at the same time? The interpretation of the derived outcome variables may no longer be the same, since it would now need to account for multiple individuals. However, the simultaneous presence of more than one consumer at an artifact would be reflected in the event transition matrix M, such that transitions previously undefined in the event network would now receive non-zero probabilities of occurring. For example, a smart shelf sensing an individual arriving twice without leaving in between would imply the presence of two different individuals standing at the shelf together; this might conceptually reflect crowding or social interaction between consumers (Argo, Dahl, & Morales, 2008; Harrell, Hutt, & Anderson, 1980).

4. Empirical Study

4.1 Data

To validate our proposed methodology, we collected non-tracking event data on in-store consumer behavior during a week-long, randomized field study using interactive, sensor-enabled display shelves. The event data fundamentally captured the interaction of consumers with products displayed on these shelves. In the following, we describe the study design, which aims to give us sufficient flexibility to demonstrate various aspects of our methodology for analyzing non-tracking event data.

The study took place in the merchandise store of a large European university at the beginning of the academic year in the autumn of 2015. The store is open Monday to Friday and, as expected, virtually all of the store's customers are affiliated with the university. The store sells a typical assortment of memorabilia, ranging from small collectibles priced around 5 Euros to clothing items at about 30 Euros. We chose a university sweatshirt and a souvenir mug to represent the store's two main product categories, apparel and collectibles, respectively. Based on historical sales data, both the sweatshirt and mug exhibited a consistent sales performance of about 20-25 units/month, which meant they were among the top sellers. The chosen products were thus popular enough to ensure the generation of sufficient event data from consumer-product interaction during the study.

We partnered with a technology company to procure four identical prototypes of sensor-enabled display shelves that could be deployed in-store. The shelves were shaped as cubes of about 20 cm (8 inches) in length, height and width; this shelf size was large enough to give us flexibility in choosing different products to put on display, while being small enough to allow easy transport and handling within the store. Each sensor-enabled shelf was equipped with a distance and pressure sensor. The distance sensor could detect the arrival and departure of an entity (e.g., customer) within about 50 cm (20 inches) of the shelf. The pressure sensor was triggered whenever the object placed on the respective shelf was picked up and put down. Crucially, each sensor-enabled shelf generated non-tracking event data, since the sensors had no way of mapping an event sequence uniquely to an individual consumer.

Upon detecting a person nearby, the distance sensor could be programmed to respond in varying degrees of complexity (e.g., lighting up in a certain color, or running a product-relevant ad on a nearby in-store TV). In our study, whenever the distance sensor was triggered, the front face of the shelf would light up in a mellow blue color. We chose this blue in an effort to minimize the confounding effect of color on the effect of the sensor-based nature of the stimulus. Past research on color and marketing suggests that the mellow blue would be noticeable enough to draw the attention of nearby shoppers, but not by itself induce any further consumer-product interaction (Singh, 2006); a qualitative pre-test appeared to confirm our expectation. The lighting functionality thus served as a simple stimulus to attract the attention of a customer standing near the shelf. The dataset obtained from each sensor-enabled shelf consisted of the timestamp, shelf number and event type per observation.

Two units of each product were placed on four sensor-enabled shelves (one unit per shelf) near the center of the store; see Appendix A1 for an illustration of the store layout and arrangement of the shelves. The prominent location of the shelves ensured that they received high foot traffic during the study, which helped generate a large enough sample of product pick-ups to allow meaningful statistical analyses. To allow between-shelf identification, we randomized the product-shelf combinations every day before the store's opening hours in the interactivity phase in two ways. First, the lighting functionality of two randomly selected shelves was always kept disabled; this allowed us to separate the effects of the product type (sweatshirt or mug) and the display interactivity triggered by the sensor (light on or off). Second, the order of the shelves was randomly shuffled; this allowed us to account for the effect of shelf location on product-customer interaction. Note that, reverse causality was not a problem in our study since the sensor-based stimulus of the shelves inherently preceded the customer's interaction with the product.

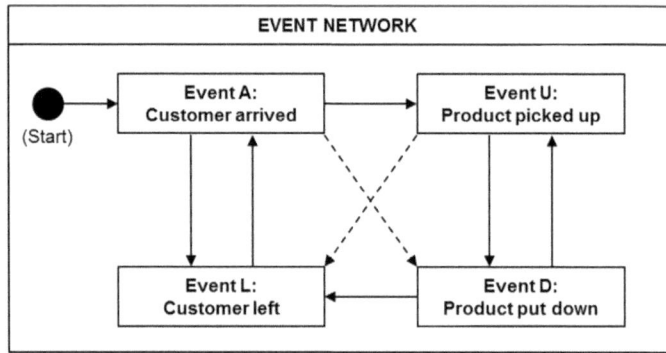

Figure 3: Event Network of Data Collected by Sensor-Enabled Shelves

In terms of the methodology described in Section 3, each unique combination of shelf interactivity (light on/off), shelf location (four locations with respect to a reference point, e.g., the checkout counter), and the type of displayed product (sweatshirt or mug) represents an artifact. Thus, the in-store event data is associated with $2 \times 4 \times 2 = 16$ possible artifacts. Four different events make up the observable event set E in relation to each artifact: "customer arrived" (A), "product picked up" (U), "product put down" (D) and "customer left" (L). The corresponding event network for a single consumer is shown in Figure 3. Notice that, for practical reasons, certain event transitions are deemed invalid (e.g., no transitions from an event to itself, and no product interaction before the consumer's arrival at the artifact is detected). The dashed arrows indicate transitions that may be valid depending on whether a consumer can remove a product from a display shelf.

VARIABLES	N	Mean	SD	Min	Max
Events					
A: Customer arrived	3016	0.471	0.499	0.000	1.000
U: Product picked up	3016	0.030	0.169	0.000	1.000
D: Product put down	3016	0.029	0.166	0.000	1.000
L: Customer left	3016	0.471	0.499	0.000	1.000
Artifact-dependent					
Shelf Location "Very Far"	3016	0.281	0.449	0.000	1.000
Shelf Location "Far"	3016	0.248	0.432	0.000	1.000
Shelf Location "Near"	3016	0.225	0.418	0.000	1.000
Shelf Location "Very Near"	3016	0.246	0.431	0.000	1.000
Product Type (1 = sweatshirt, 0 = mug)	3016	0.508	0.500	0.000	1.000
Shelf Interactivity (1 = on, 0 = off)	3016	0.491	0.500	0.000	1.000
Artifact-independent					
Time of Day (1 = before 12 pm)	3016	0.560	0.496	0.000	1.000
Day of Week (1 = before Wednesday)	3016	0.579	0.494	0.000	1.000

Note: Location variables are coded w.r.t. checkout counter

Table 2: Descriptive Statistics of Raw Event Data

Time of Day	Day of Week					Total
	Mon	Tue	Wed	Thu	Fri	
< 10 am	7	301	217	206	30	761
10 am – 12 pm	329	233	92	218	56	928
12 pm – 2 pm	206	320	92	160	48	826
> 2 pm	256	94	100	31	20	501
Total	798	948	501	615	154	3016

Table 3: Distribution of Raw Event Data over Time

Tables 2 and 3 summarize the descriptive statistics of the raw event dataset. In total, 3,016 event observations are captured. The mean values of event occurrence suggest that roughly 3% of the events involved touch-based interaction between consumers and products displayed on the sensor-enabled shelves. The means for the artifact-dependent variables reflect our randomization strategy; the observations are fairly evenly split between locations (about 25% per location), product types (about 50% each for the sweatshirt and mug), and the presence of shelf interactivity (about 50% each for shelves with lighting function enabled and disabled). Note that the location variables are coded with respect to the shelf's distance from the checkout counter. The event distribution is split roughly evenly around 12 pm (time of day), and between Monday-Tuesday and Wednesday-Friday (day of week). For simplicity, we aggregate the timestamp data into binary artifact-independent variables accordingly.

4.2 Slicing Data and Deriving Contextually-Meaningful Variables

As discussed in Section 3, we will focus on temporal slicing in paper. Based on our qualitative observation of shopper behavior and anecdotal evidence from the store assistant, individual consumers tended to stay at a given shelf for about 1 minute on average. As such, our guided approach to slicing will partition the full event stream into minute-long slices, which happens to yield 91 slices, each approximating an individual consumer. Note that in the guided approach, the number of events per slice may vary depending on the frequency of event occurrence; if several events are "bunched" together temporally, then they might all be included in the same slice. In our sample, each slice contains about 3 events ($\sigma = 3.72$), with about 22% of the slices containing at least 4 events (i.e., potentially enough to record each of the four different event types at least once for a given consumer).

We now construct outcome variables from composite conditions. While there are a number of outcomes that we could consider, in this paper we focus on three conceptual outcome variables in particular: touch, re-evaluation, and purchase. Touch refers to the propensity of consumers to physically interact with the product, which in our case means picking up the product from the shelf. A growing stream of literature argues that touch – which is inherently an often underused sensory modality – should receive more attention from retailers in order to better understand consumer behavior with respect the product offerings (Grohmann, Spangenberg, & Sprott, 2007; Krishna, 2012; Peck & Childers, 2008). The work of these authors also suggests that re-evaluating a product by touching it more than once may be a useful outcome variable to measure in an in-store context; repeated touch interactions may signify a greater interest in the product and an improved ability to evaluate the product. Finally, although we cannot directly observe product purchases in the event data, a contextually meaningful proxy may be to track the probability of a product being removed from a shelf for an unusually long period of time. In such cases, when a "put down" event is finally observed, the store assistant's anecdotal evidence suggests that this is most likely due to a new copy of the product being placed on the vacant shelf. Thus, we can plausibly infer that the removed product may have either been misplaced or in fact purchased by a customer. The underlying assumption here is that the product copy displayed on the sensor-enabled shelf can indeed be bought by a customer, i.e., it is not just for show.

Table 4 summarizes the composite conditions for each of the three outcome variables, distinguishing between weak and strong conditions. Weak conditions should be easier to satisfy than strong conditions. For example, the conceptual outcome of "touch" is – in the sense of the event data – captured by event transitions in which a touch-related event, i.e., U ("product picked up") or D ("product put down"), follows a customer's arrival (A) or precedes a customer's departure (L) from the artifact. Checking whether these event transitions occur at least once, i.e., $(P(U|A) + P(D|A) > 0) \vee (P(L|U) + P(L|D) > 0)$, amounts to a weak condition. By contrast, a strong condition would further require the probability of these touch-based event transitions to be greater than that of $P(L|A)$, which reflects a customer visit that does not involve touching the product. Similarly, the "re-evaluation" conditions capture the notion of repeated touch. The "purchase" conditions approximate the sequence of a customer's moves in which a product is picked up but not put back down by the same customer (i.e., in the same time slice).

Outcome Variables	Composite Conditions
Touch	Weak Condition: $(P(U|A) + P(D|A) > 0) \vee (P(L|U) + P(L|D) > 0)$
	Strong Condition: $\big(P(U|A) + P(D|A) > P(L|A)\big) \vee \big(P(L|U) + P(L|D) > P(L|A)\big)$
Re-evaluation	Weak Condition: $P(U|D) > 0$
	Strong Condition: $\big(P(U|D) > P(L|D)\big) \vee \big(P(U|D) > P(U|A)\big)$
Purchase	Weak Condition: $(P(D|A) > 0) \vee (P(L|U) > 0)$
	Strong Condition: $\big(P(D|A) > P(L|A)\big) \vee \big(P(L|U) > P(L|A)\big)$

Table 4: Mapping Outcome Variables to Composite Conditions

Each composite condition can now be analyzed as a binary outcome on its own, or the weak/strong condition pairs can be combined to form ordinal outcome variables. For example, in our dataset, the weak and strong conditions for "touch" are each satisfied 64 and 52 times, respectively; the weak condition alone is satisfied 12 times. Thus, we can derive an ordinal, three-level variable for "touch", coded 0 (if weak and strong conditions are both unsatisfied), 1 (if the weak condition alone is satisfied), and 2 (if the strong condition is also satisfied). The same can be done for the variables "re-evaluation" and "purchase". Note that we never have a situation where the strong condition is satisfied but the weak condition is not; this ensures the internal consistency of the ordinal outcome variable.

From the event data, we can now derive predictors that are independent of – or dependent on – artifacts. Table 2 shows the predictors that essentially emerge from the raw event data itself. The artifact-independent predictors in our data are time-related and we expect these to be contextually relevant. A consumer's in-store behavior may be constrained by out-of-store factors (e.g., shopping goals, demographics) that are captured to some extent by the time of day and/or the day of the week of the store visit (Chandon, Hutchinson, Bradlow, & Young, 2009). Meanwhile, the raw artifact-dependent predictors are:

- *Shelf location:* Previous research suggests that shelf location may affect customer-product interaction (Irion, Lu, Al-Khayyal, & Tsao, 2011; Russell & Urban, 2010). Some studies have also found that shoppers may avoid hovering sales assistants, implying a preference for unobserved buying (Kukar-Kinney, Ridgway and Monroe 2009). To see the impact of this in our experimental setting, we code the locations of the four sensor-enabled shelves based on their distance from the checkout counter where the store assistant tends to be (e.g., "very far", "far", "near", "very near").
- *Product type:* Tactile product attributes such as texture and thickness are known to affect a consumer's desire to touch the product (Grohmann et al., 2007; McCabe & Nowlis, 2003). Previous studies show that consumers react differently to simple and complex-looking products (Blijlevens, Creusen, & Schoormans, 2009). In our case, the mug would be considered fairly simple (i.e., easy to size up), whereas the sweatshirt may require additional information processing by the consumer. We may expect the sweatshirt to register more touch-related events than the mug, as consumers try to gain a better sense of the product.
- *Shelf interactivity:* Based on attentional accounts of in-store consumer behavior, the sensor-based stimulus (shelf lighting up) should attract the consumer's attention, and draw her to the product display (Baker, Parasuraman,

Grewal, & Voss, 2002; Kaltcheva & Weitz, 2006; Shankar, Inman, Mantrala, Kelley, & Rizley, 2011). Upon visiting the shelf, the consumer's attention may translate to a touch-based interaction with the product, involving re-evaluation and even purchase (Chandon et al., 2009).

As described in Section 3, we can also derive artifact-dependent predictors by constructing an artifact network. Figure 4 shows the artifact network of our in-store event dataset, generated using Python and the software Gephi (Bastian, Heymann, & Jacomy, 2009). Each node represents a unique artifact, and each artifact is coded based on its specific combination of shelf location, product type and shelf interactivity. For instance, artifact "201" is located "far" from the checkout counter (2), displays a mug (0), and the shelf interactivity (lighting) has be disabled (1). A directed edge between two artifacts reflects the fact that an event triggered at the source artifact was followed by an event triggered at the destination artifact.

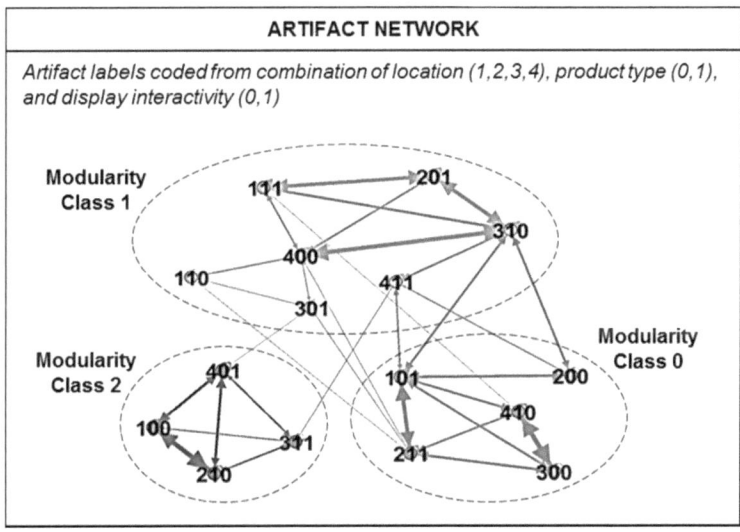

Figure 4: Artifact Network of In-Store Event Data

The artifact network allows us to derive predictors related to node centrality and its position within the network clusters (Newman, 2010; Wasserman & Faust, 1994). *Weighted degree centrality* and *eigenvector centrality* are two metrics that capture the "influence" of a node in a network. Intuitively, the influence of a node increases with the number of connections. For demonstration purposes, we do not differentiate between incoming and outgoing edges. *Betweenness centrality* captures the notion of "bridge building" between different network clusters; in our context, customer-product interactions at artifacts with a high betweenness centrality would thus intersperse interactions with other artifacts. Finally, the *modularity class* of a node reflects the cluster of the network a node is likely to belong to, beyond what would be expected in a random graph (Blondel, Guillaume, Lambiotte, & Lefebvre, 2008). Intuitively, computing the modularity class of each node and then grouping the nodes by class enables detection of notionally similar nodes. Hierarchical clustering is an alternative approach for detecting communities of similar nodes in networks (Newman, 2010). Formal definitions of the above network measures are given in Appendix A2.

4.3 Results

VARIABLES	N	Mean	SD	Min	Max
Outcomes (2 = strong, 1 = weak, 0 = none)					
Touch	745	0.156	0.521	0.000	2.000
Re-evaluation	745	0.015	0.159	0.000	2.000
Possible Purchase	745	0.034	0.238	0.000	2.000
Predictors					
Artifact-dependent (raw)					
Shelf Location "Very Far"	745	0.281	0.450	0.000	1.000
Shelf Location "Far"	745	0.239	0.427	0.000	1.000
Shelf Location "Near"	745	0.226	0.418	0.000	1.000
Shelf Location "Very Near"	745	0.255	0.436	0.000	1.000
Product Type (1 = sweatshirt, 0 = mug)	745	0.468	0.499	0.000	1.000
Shelf Interactivity (1 = on, 0 = off)	745	0.466	0.499	0.000	1.000
Artifact-dependent (network)					
Weighted Degree Centrality	745	458.977	174.967	76.000	782.000
Eigenvector Centrality	745	0.679	0.278	0.236	1.000
Betweenness Centrality	745	23.408	20.546	0.000	44.000
Modularity Class	745	0.875	0.740	0.000	2.000
Artifact-independent					
Time of Day (1 = before 12 pm)	745	0.383	0.486	0.000	1.000
Day of Week (1 = before Wednesday)	745	0.848	0.359	0.000	1.000

Note: Location variables are coded w.r.t. checkout counter

Table 5: Descriptive Statistics of Sliced Event Data (Guided Approach)

Table 5 shows the descriptive statistics for our in-store event data, temporally sliced into 1-minute intervals using a guided approach. As a panel, the data can be grouped into 91 slices (approximating individual consumers) interacting with up to 16 artifacts. Bearing in mind that the slices are not evenly sized, we obtain 745 observations in total. We estimate negative binomial regression models for "touch" outcome, which is observed more frequently (64 times) than "re-evaluation" (7 times) and "purchase" (16 times). Table 6 shows the results of estimating full and reduced random effects regressions for "touch". For the sake of completeness, we also show the full random effects models for all three outcome variables (touch, re-evaluation and purchase) in Table 7. Note that, due to the high skewness of the re-evaluation and purchase outcomes, we employ a simple random effects OLS model to achieve model convergence for these outcomes. Also, the results of the Hausman test for each of the specifications support our use of the random effects model over the fixed effect alternative.

The presence of a sweatshirt and shelf interactivity both appear to increase the likelihood of touch. Time of day is also a significant predictor, such that consumers appear to interact with the artifacts more in the afternoon. The significant but negative coefficients for shelf location might imply a tendency towards unobserved buying (Kukar-Kinney, Ridgway, & Monroe, 2009). Moreover, although degree and betweenness centrality are positively correlated with touch, eigenvector centrality is not. This result highlights the subtle difference between the eigenvector and weighted degree centrality measures. In particular, by the nature of the essentially recursive computation, the eigenvector centrality of a node will be low if it is connected to relatively "unimportant" or non-central nodes; as the results indicate, this may be conducive to touch interaction. By contrast, weighted degree centrality is computed by taking the edge-weighted sum of the connections, regardless of the degree of the nodes in general. Finally, we also find that the modularity class (i.e., node cluster) of an artifact can affect the level of touch interaction.

Furthermore, the differences between the coefficients of the raw and network-based predictors underscore the value of taking a network perspective. Consider the artifacts depicted in Figure 4. Artifacts in modularity class 0 tend to be located farther away from the checkout counter than artifacts in the other two clusters. The negative coefficients of modularity classes 1 and 2 relative to the baseline class 0 thus suggest that the consumers in our study may have a tendency for unobserved buying. Meanwhile, artifacts that are physically close tend to be densely connected (as depicted by the thickness of the corresponding edges in Figure 4), suggesting that a consumer is likely to interact with products displayed on adjacent shelves. The thickest edges in the network appear between artifacts that have the same shelf interactivity setting (either both have lighting on or both have it off), but different product types. These qualitative observations are reflected in regression results in

Tables 6 and 7, and the network perspective thus arguably allows for a more nuanced interpretation of the raw predictors.

	Outcome Variable: Touch		
PREDICTORS	Model 1a [N]	Model 1b [N]	Model 1 [N]
Artifact-dependent (raw)			
Shelf Location "Very Far" [L]	-0.192		0.347
	[0.334]		[0.518]
Shelf Location "Far" [L]	-0.665*		0.067
	[0.369]		[0.526]
Shelf Location "Near" [L]	-0.240		-0.688*
	[0.358]		[0.386]
Product Type (1 = sweatshirt, 0 = mug)	0.983***		1.082***
	[0.269]		[0.302]
Shelf Interactivity (1 = on, 0 = off)	0.768***		-0.248
	[0.272]		[0.556]
Artifact-dependent (network)			
Weighted Degree Centrality		0.005**	0.005**
		[0.002]	[0.002]
Eigenvector Centrality		-9.250***	-10.995**
		[2.944]	[4.718]
Betweenness Centrality		0.051***	0.072**
		[0.016]	[0.033]
Modularity Class 1 [M]		-0.707	-1.196
		[0.552]	[0.789]
Modularity Class 2 [M]		-3.171**	-3.992*
		[1.355]	[2.227]
Artifact-independent			
Time of Day (1 = before 12 pm)	1.194***	1.182***	1.165***
	[0.293]	[0.298]	[0.299]
Day of Week (1 = before Wednesday)	-0.049	-0.260	-0.371
	[0.521]	[0.558]	[0.565]
Constant	-3.569***	1.069	1.728
	[0.564]	[1.553]	[2.505]
Wald X^2	45.99***	44.07***	63.92***
Observations	745	745	745
Number of Groups (Artifacts)	16	16	16

Standard errors in brackets
*** p<0.01, ** p<0.05, * p<0.1
[N] Model uses negative binomial regression
[L] Base shelf location is "Very Near"; location variables are coded w.r.t. checkout counter
[M] Base modularity class is 0

Table 6: Random Effects Models of "Touch" Outcome

| | Outcome Variables | | |
PREDICTORS	Touch Model 1 [N]	Re-evaluation Model 2	Purchase Model 3
Artifact-dependent (raw)			
Shelf Location "Very Far" [L]	0.347	-0.027	-0.013
	[0.518]	[0.029]	[0.049]
Shelf Location "Far" [L]	0.067	-0.020	-0.013
	[0.526]	[0.030]	[0.050]
Shelf Location "Near" [L]	-0.688*	-0.075***	-0.080*
	[0.386]	[0.029]	[0.048]
Product Type (1 = sweatshirt, 0 = mug)	1.082***	0.018	0.002
	[0.302]	[0.016]	[0.028]
Shelf Interactivity (1 = on, 0 = off)	-0.248	-0.010	-0.005
	[0.556]	[0.037]	[0.061]
Artifact-dependent (network)			
Weighted Degree Centrality	0.005**	0.000	0.000
	[0.002]	[0.000]	[0.000]
Eigenvector Centrality	-10.995**	-0.433	-0.581
	[4.718]	[0.267]	[0.437]
Betweenness Centrality	0.072**	0.003	0.004
	[0.033]	[0.002]	[0.003]
Modularity Class 1 [M]	-1.196	-0.043	-0.022
	[0.789]	[0.035]	[0.058]
Modularity Class 2 [M]	-3.992*	-0.185	-0.242
	[2.227]	[0.126]	[0.206]
Artifact-independent			
Time of Day (1 = before 12 pm)	1.165***	0.037***	0.007
	[0.299]	[0.013]	[0.020]
Day of Week (1 = before Wednesday)	-0.371	-0.008	0.021
	[0.565]	[0.019]	[0.029]
Constant	1.728	0.226	0.282
	[2.505]	[0.142]	[0.231]
Wald X^2	63.92***	24.33**	10.52
Observations	745	745	745
Number of Groups (Artifacts)	16	16	16

Standard errors in brackets
*** p<0.01, ** p<0.05, * p<0.1
[N] Model uses negative binomial regression (rest of the models use OLS regression)
[L] Base shelf location is "Very Near"; location variables coded w.r.t. checkout counter
[M] Base modularity class is 0

Table 7: Full Random Effects Models of Outcome Variables

5. Conclusion and Discussion

With the increasing digitization of the retail industry, there is a growing abundance of data on consumer behavior (McAfee & Brynjolfsson, 2012; Rigby, 2011). In particular, advances in sensor-based and mobile technology have allowed retailers to track consumers at the individual level in online and offline settings using event-based data formats (Shankar et al., 2011). In essence, a stream of event data captures a sequence of events that reflect actions taken by the consumer in various scenarios (e.g., browsing online, traveling to/between stores, movement inside a store). Recent literature has led to some important insights by looking at event data that tracks individuals or sensor-enabled devices on their person (Hui et al., 2009b; Larson et al., 2005). At the same time, a large portion of the event data being generated by devices cannot be matched exactly to individual consumers, providing a wealth of fragmented and unstructured "non-tracking event data" (Porter & Heppelmann, 2014, 2015). As evidenced by the recent calls for research, scholars and practitioners are increasingly recognizing the need for methods that can analyzing event data in retail (Grewal et al., 2016; Wedel & Kannan, 2016).

Non-tracking event data is fraught with two central challenges: (1) the inability to track individual consumers, and (2) the difficulty of deriving contextually meaningful outcome variables and explanatory variables for predictive analyses. In this paper, we respond to the related calls for research, and the relative lack of retail marketing literature that directly addresses the abovementioned challenges of non-tracking event data, by making three interrelated methodological contributions. First, we classify event data by the retail context (online, between-store and in-store) and type of event data (tracking and non-tracking) to get a better sense of the existing work on event data, and grasp the challenges posed by non-tracking event data. Second, we leverage the existing conceptual work on "path data" (Hui et al., 2009a) to develop a methodology for structuring and analyzing non-tracking event data. Third, we test the methodology using a dataset generated from sensor-enabled shelves deployed in the context of an in-store field experiment.

Our methodology fundamentally aims to achieve the following complementary goals: (1) making sense of non-tracking event data by approximating individuals and deriving contextually meaningful variables, (2) being flexible enough to allow application to a range of retail scenarios involving non-tracking event data, and (3) facilitate adoption in practice by allowing retailers to integrate the methodology into existing technical infrastructure. Based on the operationalization and results, we would argue that the empirical study validates our proposed methodology. By slicing event data along one or more dimensions (e.g., time or space) using a guided or unguided approach, we show that it may be possible to approximately identify individuals. Moreover, by taking a network perspective of events and the artifacts at which they are generated (e.g., a smart shelf), we demonstrate ways to derive contextually meaningful variables; outcome variables can be constructed by applying composite conditions to event transition probabilities, while useful predictors can come either directly from the raw data or via a network analysis of the artifacts. Taken together, slicing and network analysis allow us to make sense of the event data across a range of retail settings by recasting it as a panel of individuals interacting with artifacts. The modular nature of the methodology and using a combination of otherwise well-known "building blocks" (e.g., network measures, regression models) means that data scientists can in practice modify and extend our work to suit their specific needs.

The work presented in this paper has some interesting implications for marketing research. Bradlow et al. (2017) argue that the revolution in retail surrounding the much-hyped notion of "big data" is really about "better data", and how novel data analysis techniques can be informed by marketing theory to deliver useful insights. We complement the approach of Bradlow et al. by looking at the untapped potential of non-tracking event streams. With the growth in pervasive computing, researchers will increasingly have access to mobile and sensor-enabled technology that can fairly cheaply capture data that is "long" (lots of observations or rows) but not necessarily able to track individual consumers. The methodology demonstrated in this paper suggests that non-tracking data may indeed lead to useful insights in retail. Our approach also implies that scholars should pay more attention to the value of the network perspective. Borgatti et al. (2009) described the use of network analysis in the social sciences, but most of the extant applications tend to look at networks of people, whether at the individual or institutional level. By considering networks of events and artifacts, our work sheds some light on the largely unexplored notion in marketing research of nodes that represent aggregate behaviors of agents outside the network boundary (Dhar et al., 2014). Our approach to deriving outcome and predictor variables also reflects the use of "multi-level" networks; the event-level nodes yield the outcome variables, while the artifact-level nodes yield the predictors.

The proposed methodology for analyzing non-tracking event data also has important managerial implications. Firstly, retail managers and data analysts should not ignore the vast amounts of event data that cannot be exactly mapped to individual consumers. Although many retailers are beginning to adopt sensor-based technology for "back-end" optimization (e.g., improving inventory planning and logistics) (Gorshe et al., 2012; Moon & Ngai, 2008), our conversations with store managers in the consumer goods and fashion segments suggest that there has been limited progress in certain aspects of "front-end" analytics (e.g., using sensors to understand how consumers interact with products in a store). We demonstrate a set of modular steps (slicing, deriving variables, and building models) that retailers can follow to make sense of the non-tracking event data generated by consumers across a range of online and offline contexts. Secondly, the network perspective shown in this paper can be combined with standard (experimental) A/B testing techniques to derive a more holistic set of contextually relevant measures of retail performance (Martin & Hanington, 2012). For example, whether they are assessing the effectiveness of a website or a store's atmosphere, retail analysts can consider the use of event networks in deriving meaningful outcome variables. Moreover, in assessing the value of a store's artifacts, one can look at not just the raw attributes of the artifacts but also their notional centrality and position in the artifact network.

The methodology presented in this paper has two main limitations. First, while the use of a slicing heuristic can help approximately separate the events attributable to different individuals, it does not let us detect repeat visits by the same individual. In the empirical study, for example, we have no way of telling whether a certain consumer interacted with the products on multiple days. Each slice of the event stream is implicitly treated as different and independent individual. Discerning this particular case of interaction between consumers and artifacts from non-tracking event data alone may be generally intractable, and would arguably necessitate some outside insight in practice (e.g., past experience, qualitative observation). Secondly, there may be – at least in a managerial sense – a conceptual limit to the interpretability of variables generated from composite conditions and network measures. Conditions composed of more than four or five transition probabilities may become too difficult to grasp in practice, and the numerous variations on the measures of node centrality and network structure – e.g., see Newman (2010) – may be difficult to always translate into managerially relevant insights. As such, our methodology could serve as a starting point for thinking about non-tracking event data, and a complementary approach to other related frameworks of analysis (Hui et al., 2009a).

Future work can address the limitations of the methodology and its validation. One could explore more sophisticated methods of slicing, and validate our approach in other retail scenarios (e.g., online and between-store). Beyond this, we outline one novel extension of our work in more detail. Specifically, retailers make investments across the customer journey (Lemon & Verhoef, 2016), but the success of these investments is often predicated on consumers interfacing with the retailers' touch-points (e.g., website, store) in certain ways. For example, store layouts may be optimized to steer consumers towards certain product categories, but this is useless if the consumers do not go through the intended motions (e.g., visiting a given aisle, picking up a product and so on) (Shankar et al., 2011). In terms of the conceptual event network depicted in Figure 2a, the notion of "going through the motions" amounts to what we might call "interaction loops". An interaction loop is defined as a sequence of events that begins with a consumer arriving at an artifact (e.g., landing on a webpage, visiting a shelf), involves some interaction with the given artifact, and ends with the consumer leaving the artifact. While we have only considered transition probabilities of the form $P(e_j|e_i)$ in this paper, the study of interaction loops might involve "chaining" several of these transition probabilities. Operationally, we could then go on to construct outcome variables representing the occurrence and length of interaction loops, and analyze the impact of various contextual predictors.

Appendix

A1. Store Layout in Field Study

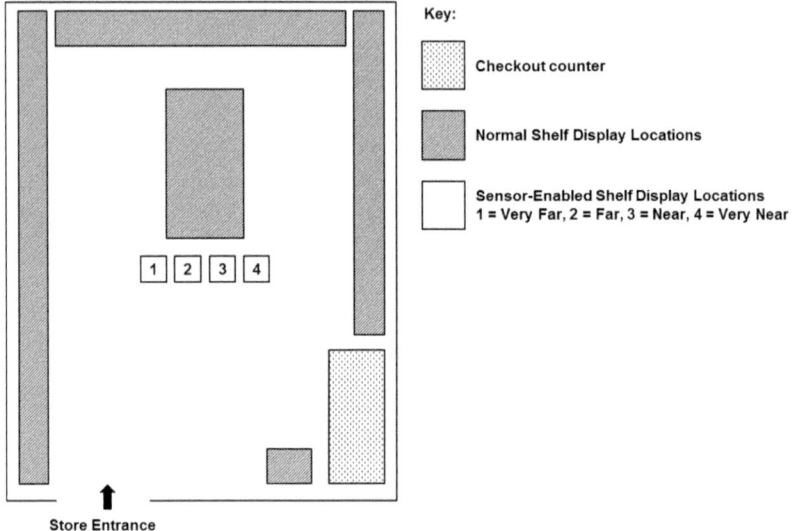

Figure A1.1: Illustration of Store Layout in Field Study

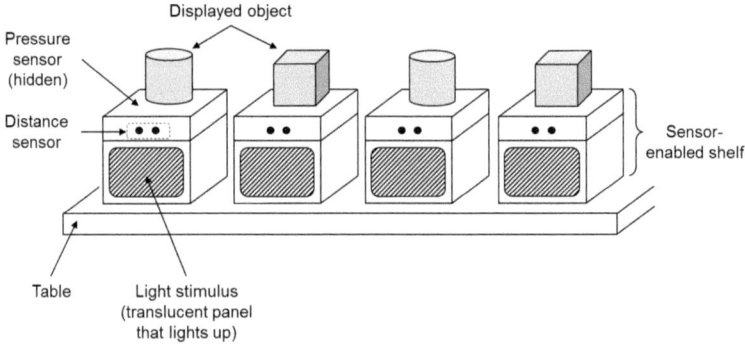

Figure A1.2: Illustration of Sensor-Enabled Shelves in a Row

A2. Formal Definitions of Network Measures

We describe the formalizations in terms of a network $G = (V, E)$ with $|V|$ nodes and $|E|$ edges. The network can equally be described by a weighted matrix W, such that the element W_{ij} represents the strength of the edge between nodes i and j (e.g., frequency of co-occurrences in the case of event data). Let the adjacency matrix A_{ij} denote a non-weighted version of W_{ij}, such that the element $A_{ij} = 1$ if nodes i and j are connected and 0 otherwise. Below are the typical definitions of network measures used in our paper (Newman, 2010; Opsahl, Agneessens, & Skvoretz, 2010; Wasserman & Faust, 1994):

- **Weighted Degree Centrality** $C_D{}^W$ of node i: $C_D{}^W(i) = \sum_j^{|V|} W_{ij}$
- **Eigenvector Centrality** C_E of node i: $C_E(i) = \frac{1}{\lambda} \sum_j^{|V|} A_{ij} C_E(j)$, where λ is the largest eigenvalue of A_{ij}.
- **Betweenness Centrality** C_B of node i: $C_B(i) = \frac{g_{jk}(i)}{g_{jk}}$, where g_{jk} denotes the number of shortest paths between nodes j and k, and $g_{jk}(i)$ of these paths go via node i.
- **Modularity Class** c of node i: The modularity of a network partition is given by $Q = \frac{1}{2m} \sum_{i,j} \left[W_{ij} - \frac{k_i k_j}{2m} \right] \delta(c_i, c_j)$, where $k_i = \sum_j W_{ij}$, c_i is the modularity class (or network community/cluster) to which node i is assigned, $\delta(c_i, c_j) = 1$ if $c_i = c_j$ and 0 otherwise, and $m = \frac{1}{2} \sum_{ij} W_{ij}$.

References

Aguirre, E., Mahr, D., Grewal, D., Ruyter, K. de, & Wetzels, M. (2015). Unraveling the personalization paradox: The effect of information collection and trust-building strategies on online advertisement effectiveness. *Journal of Retailing, 91*(1), 34–49.

Argo, J. J., Dahl, D. W., & Morales, A. C. (2008). Positive consumer contagion: Responses to attractive others in a retail context. *Journal of Marketing Research, 45*(6), 690–701.

Baker, J., Parasuraman, A., Grewal, D., & Voss, G. B. (2002). The influence of multiple store environment cues on perceived merchandise value and patronage intentions. *Journal of Marketing, 66*(2), 120–141.

Bastian, M., Heymann, S., & Jacomy, M. (2009). Gephi: an open source software for exploring and manipulating networks. *ICWSM, 8*, 361–362.

Batten, N. (2012). *Burberry Regent Street pilots interactive technology.* Retrieved from http://www.marketingmagazine.co.uk/article/1149851/burberry-regent-street-pilots-interactive-technology

Blijlevens, J., Creusen, M. E. H., & Schoormans, J. P. L. (2009). How consumers perceive product appearance: The identification of three product appearance attributes. *International Journal of Design, 3*(3).

Blondel, V. D., Guillaume, J.-L., Lambiotte, R., & Lefebvre, E. (2008). Fast unfolding of communities in large networks. *Journal of statistical mechanics: theory and experiment, 2008*(10), P10008.

Borgatti, S. P., Mehra, A., Brass, D. J., & Labianca, G. (2009). Network analysis in the social sciences. *Science, 323*(5916), 892–895.

Bradlow, E. T., Gangwar, M., Kopalle, P., & Voleti, S. (2017). The Role of Big Data and Predictive Analytics in Retailing. *Journal of Retailing, 93*(1), 79–95.

Bucklin, R. E., & Sismeiro, C. (2009). Click here for Internet insight: Advances in clickstream data analysis in marketing. *Journal of Interactive Marketing, 23*(1), 35–48.

Bughin, J., Chui, M., & Manyika, J. (2015). An executive's guide to the Internet of Things. *McKinsey Quarterly, 2*(9), 89–105.

Burke, R. R. (2010). The third wave of marketing intelligence. In *Retailing in the 21st Century* (pp. 159–171). Springer.

Chandon, P., Hutchinson, J. W., Bradlow, E. T., & Young, S. H. (2009). Does in-store marketing work? Effects of the number and position of shelf facings on brand attention and evaluation at the point of purchase. *Journal of Marketing, 73*(6), 1–17.

Cox, D. R., & Isham, V. (1980). *Point processes. Monographs on statistics and applied probability: Vol. 12.* Boca Raton, Fla.: Chapman & Hall/CRC.

Cox, N. (2007). Stata tip 43: Remainders, selections, sequences, extractions: Uses of the modulus. *Stata Journal, 7*(1), 143–145.

Dhar, V., Geva, T., Oestreicher-Singer, G., & Sundararajan, A. (2014). Prediction in economic networks. *Information Systems Research, 25*(2), 264–284.

Diebold, F. X. (2012). On the Origin(s) and Development of the Term 'Big Data'.

Drèze, X., & Hussherr, F.-X. (2003). Internet advertising: Is anybody watching? *Journal of Interactive Marketing, 17*(4), 8–23.

Ghose, A., & Yang, S. (2009). An empirical analysis of search engine advertising: Sponsored search in electronic markets. *Management Science, 55*(10), 1605–1622.

Gorshe, M., Rollman, M., & Beverly, R. (2012). Item-Level RFID: A Competitive Differentiator.

Granbois, D. H. (1968). Improving the study of customer in-store behavior. *The Journal of Marketing,* 28–33.

Grewal, D., Roggeveen, A., & Nordfält, J. (2016). The Future of Retailing. *Journal of Retailing, 93*(1), 1–6.

Grohmann, B., Spangenberg, E. R., & Sprott, D. E. (2007). The influence of tactile input on the evaluation of retail product offerings. *Journal of Retailing, 83*(2), 237–245.

Guralnik, V., & Srivastava, J. (1999). Event detection from time series data. In *Proceedings of the fifth ACM SIGKDD international conference on Knowledge discovery and data mining* (pp. 33–42).

Harrell, G. D., Hutt, M. D., & Anderson, J. C. (1980). Path analysis of buyer behavior under conditions of crowding. *Journal of Marketing Research,* (17), 45–51.

Hausman, J. A. (1978). Specification tests in econometrics. *Econometrica: Journal of the Econometric Society,* 1251–1271.

Hui, S. K., Bradlow, E. T., & Fader, P. S. (2009). Testing behavioral hypotheses using an integrated model of grocery store shopping path and purchase behavior. *Journal of Consumer Research, 36*(3), 478–493.

Hui, S. K., Fader, P. S., & Bradlow, E. T. (2009a). Path data in marketing: An integrative framework and prospectus for model building. *Marketing Science, 28*(2), 320–335.

Hui, S. K., Fader, P. S., & Bradlow, E. T. (2009b). The traveling salesman goes shopping: The systematic deviations of grocery paths from TSP optimality. *Marketing Science, 28*(3), 566–572.

Hui, S. K., Inman, J. J., Huang, Y., & Suher, J. (2013). The effect of in-store travel distance on unplanned spending: Applications to mobile promotion strategies. *Journal of Marketing, 77*(2), 1–16.

Ilfeld, J. S., & Winer, R. S. (2002). Generating website traffic. *Journal of Advertising Research, 42*(5), 49–61.

Inman, J., & Nikolova, H. (2017). Shopper-Facing Retail Technology: A Retailer Adoption Decision Framework Incorporating Shopper Attitudes and Privacy Concerns, *93*(1), 7–28.

Irion, J., Lu, J.-C., Al-Khayyal, F. A., & Tsao, Y.-C. (2011). A hierarchical decomposition approach to retail shelf space management and assortment decisions. *Journal of the Operational Research Society, 62*(10), 1861–1870.

Kaltcheva, V. D., & Weitz, B. A. (2006). When should a retailer create an exciting store environment? *Journal of Marketing, 70*(1), 107–118.

Kimball, R., & Ross, M. (2009). *The data warehouse toolkit: The complete guide to dimensional modeling* (2nd ed.). New York: Wiley.

Krishna, A. (2012). An integrative review of sensory marketing: Engaging the senses to affect perception, judgment and behavior. *Journal of Consumer Psychology, 22*(3), 332–351.

Kukar-Kinney, M., Ridgway, N. M., & Monroe, K. B. (2009). The relationship between consumers' tendencies to buy compulsively and their motivations to shop and buy on the Internet. *Journal of Retailing, 85*(3), 298–307.

Kumar, R., Mahadevan, U., & Sivakumar, D. (2004). A graph-theoretic approach to extract storylines from search results. In *Proceedings of the tenth ACM SIGKDD international conference on Knowledge discovery and data mining* (pp. 216–225).

Larson, J. S., Bradlow, E. T., & Fader, P. S. (2005). An exploratory look at supermarket shopping paths. *International Journal of Research in Marketing, 22*(4), 395–414.

Lemon, K. N., & Verhoef, P. C. (2016). Understanding customer experience throughout the customer journey. *Journal of Marketing, 80*(6), 69–96.

Li, H., & Kannan, P. K. (2014). Attributing conversions in a multichannel online marketing environment: An empirical model and a field experiment. *Journal of Marketing Research, 51*(1), 40–56.

Luo, X., Andrews, M., Fang, Z., & Phang, C. W. (2013). Mobile targeting. *Management Science, 60*(7), 1738–1756.

Martin, B., & Hanington, B. M. (2012). *Universal methods of design*. Beverly, MA: Rockport Publishers.

Mazze, E. M. (1974). Determining shopper movement patterns by cognitive maps. *Journal of Retailing, 50*(3), 43–48.

McAfee, A., & Brynjolfsson, E. (2012). Big data: The management revolution. *Harvard Business Review, 90*(10), 61–67.

McCabe, D. B., & Nowlis, S. M. (2003). The effect of examining actual products or product descriptions on consumer preference. *Journal of Consumer Psychology, 13*(4), 431–439.

Miyazaki, A. D. (2008). Online privacy and the disclosure of cookie use: Effects on consumer trust and anticipated patronage. *Journal of Public Policy & Marketing, 27*(1), 19–33.

Molitor, D., Reichhart, P., Spann, M., & Ghose, A. (2016). Measuring the effectiveness of location-based advertising: A randomized field experiment.

Montgomery, A. L., Li, S., Srinivasan, K., & Liechty, J. C. (2004). Modeling online browsing and path analysis using clickstream data. *Marketing Science, 23*(4), 579–595.

Moon, K. L., & Ngai, E. W. (2008). The adoption of RFID in fashion retailing: A business value-added framework. *Industrial Management & Data Systems, 108*(5), 596–612.

Nagarajan, M., Gomadam, K., Sheth, A. P., Ranabahu, A., Mutharaju, R., & Jadhav, A. (2009). Spatio-temporal-thematic analysis of citizen sensor data: Challenges and experiences. In *International Conference on Web Information Systems Engineering* (pp. 539–553).

Newman, M. (2010). *Networks: An Introduction* (9th ed.). Oxford: Oxford University Press.

Opsahl, T., Agneessens, F., & Skvoretz, J. (2010). Node centrality in weighted networks: Generalizing degree and shortest paths. *Social Networks, 32*(3), 245–251.

Peck, J., & Childers, T. L. (2008). Sensory factors and consumer behavior. *Handbook of Consumer Psychology,* 193–219.

Pennacchioli, D., Coscia, M., Rinzivillo, S., Pedreschi, D., & Giannotti, F. (2013). Explaining the product range effect in purchase data. In *2013 IEEE International Conference on Big Data* (pp. 648–656).

Phua, P., Page, B., & Bogomolova, S. (2015). Validating Bluetooth logging as metric for shopper behaviour studies. *Journal of Retailing and Consumer Services, 22,* 158–163.

Pieters, R., & Warlop, L. (1999). Visual attention during brand choice: The impact of time pressure and task motivation. *International Journal of Research in Marketing, 16*(1), 1–16.

Porter, M. E., & Heppelmann, J. E. (2014). How smart, connected products are transforming competition. *Harvard Business Review, 92*(11), 64–88.

Porter, M. E., & Heppelmann, J. E. (2015). How smart, connected products are transforming companies. *Harvard Business Review, 93*(10), 96–114.

Rafaeli, A., Altman, D., Gremler, D. D., Huang, M.-H., Grewal, D., Iyer, B., . . . Ruyter, K. de. (2017). The Future of Frontline Research: Invited Commentaries. *Journal of Service Research, 20*(1), 91–99.

Rigby, D. (2011). The future of shopping. *Harvard Business Review, 89*(12), 65–76.

Russell, R. A., & Urban, T. L. (2010). The location and allocation of products and product families on retail shelves. *Annals of Operations Research, 179*(1), 131–147.

Russo, J. E., & Leclerc, F. (1994). An eye-fixation analysis of choice processes for consumer nondurables. *Journal of Consumer Research, 21*(2), 274–290.

Savchenko, I., & Gatsenko, O. Y. (2015). Analytical review of methods of providing internet anonymity. *Automatic Control and Computer Sciences, 49*(8), 696–700.

Shankar, V., Inman, J. J., Mantrala, M., Kelley, E., & Rizley, R. (2011). Innovations in shopper marketing: current insights and future research issues. *Journal of Retailing, 87,* S29-S42.

Sherman, L., & Deighton, J. (2001). Banner advertising: Measuring effectiveness and optimizing placement. *Journal of Interactive Marketing, 15*(2), 60–64.

Shi, S. W., Wedel, M., & Pieters, F. G. (2013). Information acquisition during online decision making: A model-based exploration using eye-tracking data. *Management Science, 59*(5), 1009–1026.

Singh, S. (2006). Impact of color on marketing. *Management Decision, 44*(6), 783–789.

Sismeiro, C., & Bucklin, R. E. (2004). Modeling purchase behavior at an e-commerce web site: A task-completion approach. *Journal of Marketing Research, 41*(3), 306–323.

Sorensen, H., Bogomolova, S., Anderson, K., Trinh, G., Sharp, A., Kennedy, R., . . . Wright, M. (2017). Fundamental patterns of in-store shopper behavior. *Journal of Retailing and Consumer Services, 37,* 182–194.

Tellis, G. (2004). *Effective Advertising.* Thousand Oaks, CA: Sage.

Underhill, P. (2000). *Why We Buy: The Science of Shopping* (1st Touchstone ed.). New York, Toronto: Simon & Schuster.

Varian, H. R. (2014). Big data: New tricks for econometrics. *The Journal of Economic Perspectives, 28*(2), 3–27.

Wang, J. (2013). *Handbook of finite state based models and applications. Discrete mathematics and its applications.* Boca Raton: CRC Press.

Wasserman, S., & Faust, K. (1994). *Social Network Analysis: Methods and Applications. Structural analysis in the social sciences: Vol. 8.* Cambridge: Cambridge University Press.

Wedel, M., & Kannan, P. K. (2016). Marketing analytics for data-rich environments. *Journal of Marketing, 80*(6), 97–121.

Wooldridge, J. (2013). *Introductory Econometrics: A Modern Approach* (5th ed.). Ohio: South-Western.

Xu, L., Duan, J. A., & Whinston, A. (2014). Path to purchase: A mutually exciting point process model for online advertising and conversion. *Management Science, 60*(6), 1392–1412.

Yang, Y., Pierce, T., & Carbonell, J. (1998). A study of retrospective and on-line event detection. In *Proceedings of the 21st annual international ACM SIGIR conference on Research and development in information retrieval* (pp. 28–36).